CHARLEY CRAFT

The Life and Times of a North Carolinian
Turned Oklahoma Homesteader, 1872-1934

by

Neal G. Lineback

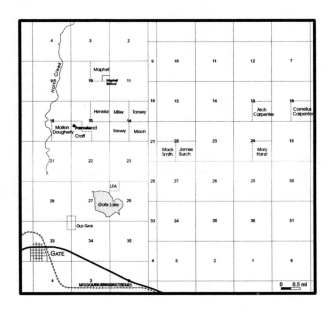

Gate, OK

Library of Congress Cataloging-in-Publication Data

Lineback, Neal G.
   Charley Craft : the life and times of a North Carolinian
turned Oklanhoma homesteader, 1872-1934 / Neal G. Lineback.
       p. cm.
   Summary: "Charley and Martha Craft homesteaded 120
acres of raw, dusty prairie in the Oklahoma Panhandle in
1905. It was a difficult place to raise a family of six children
as tornadoes, droughts, hailstorms, and blizzards made their
lives more difficult." -- Provided by publisher.
   Includes bibliograhical references and index.
   1. Craft, Charley, 1872-1934. 2. Craft Family. 3. Pio-
neers--Oklahoma--Oklahoma Panhandle--Biography 4.
Oklahoma Panhandle (Okla.)--Biography. 5. Oklahoma
Panhandle (Okla.)--Social life and customs. I. Title.
F702.N6L56 2005
976.6'13'092--dc22

2005019065

Book and Cover Design by: Gina K. Cavallaro

Dedicated

With Affection and Appreciation to
The Charles Vachel and Martha Newby Craft Family,
and particularly to
Harold, Velma, Maurie, Buelah, and Jeanne

Contents

LIST OF FIGURES

LIST OF TABLES

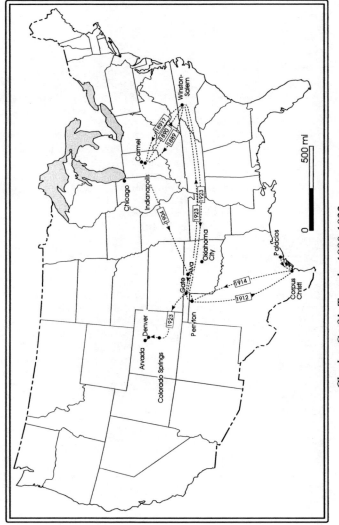

Charley Craft's Travels, 1890-1932.

Abbreviated Family Tree
Charles Vachel Craft (Charley Craft) 1-7-1

1.Vachel Craft
(m) Mary S. Payne
(12 Children)
1-1 Theresa M. Craft
1-2 Stephen Winburn Craft
1-3 Nathan L. Craft
1-4 Albert W. Craft
1-5 Mary Amelia Craft
1-6 James Calvin Craft
1-7 Junius Irving Craft
1-8 Cynthia Leah Craft
1-9 Sarah E. Craft
1-10 William Luther Craft
1-11 Senia Ellen Craft
1-12 John Tillet Craft

1-7 Junius Irving Craft
(m) Jane Harriet Kimel
(1Child)
1-7-1 Charles Vachel Craft
(Charley Craft)

1-7-1 Charles Vachel Craft
Ellen George
(1Child)
1-7-1-1 Junius Levita George

1-7-1-1 Junius Levita George
(m) Lelia Hampton Barr
(1 Child)
1-7-1-1-1 Anne Ellen George

1-7-1-1-1 Anne Ellen George
(m) George C. Moose
(No Children)

1-7-1 Charles Vachel Craft
(m) Martha Ann Newby
(6 Children)
1-7-1-2 Paul Vachel Craft
1-7-1-3 Buelah Florina Craft
1-7-1-4 Harriet Maurie Craft
1-7-1-5 Cecil Irving Craft
1-7-1-6 Harold Newby Craft
1-7-1-7 Forrest Emmanuel Craft

1-7-1-3 Buelah Florina Craft
(m) Leslie Carpenter
(1 Child)
1-7-1-3-1 Vera Jeanne Carpenter

1-7-1-3-1 Vera Jeanne Carpenter
(m) Sidney Baker
(2 Children)

1-7 Junius Irving Craft
(m) Martha Antonette Styers
(6 Children)
1-7-2 Odella Madora Craft
1-7-3 Etta Amelia Craft
1-7-4 Virginia (Jenny) Wall Craft
1-7-.5 Daisy Estelle Craft
1-7-6 Samuel Irving Craft
1-7-7 Martha Blanche Craft

1-7-2 Odella Madora Craft
(m) Ellis Armenius Lineback
(11 Children)
1-7-2-1 Freda Estella Lineback
1-7-2-2 Eula Madora Lineback
1-7-2-3 Elmer Junius Lineback
1-7-2-4 Jasper Winburn Lineback
1-7-2-5 Mayola Katherine Lineback
1-7-2-6 Haywood Armenius Lineback
1-7-2-7 Ellis Hiatt Lineback
1-7-2-8.Frank Jefferson Lineback
1-7-2-9 Sara Antionette Lineback
1-7-2-10 Elva Lucille Lineback
1-7-2-11 Laura Mildred Lineback

1-7-3 Etta Amelia Craft
(m) William "Bill" Leinbach
(5 Children)
1-7-3-1 Mary Lois Leinbach
1-7-3-2 Treva Estelle Leinbach
1-7-3-3 Willie Winella Leinbach
1-7-3-4 Inez Virginia Leinbach
1-7-3-5 Martha Ruth Leinbach

Prologue

Charley Craft's story is a microcosm of the great American migration of the 19th and the beginning of the 20th centuries, as landless migrants and their families sought farmland to settle, often at extreme personal cost. The climate of much of the land west of the Mississippi was too dry, too harsh, and too erratic to have ever been brought under the plow. In their frantic search for "free land," families from the humid East homesteaded marginal lands, such as that of the Panhandle of Oklahoma, and endured the consequences.

Charley Craft was a rural North Carolinian born in 1872 just after the Civil War, but ostracized by his own community. He left North Carolina for Indiana in 1889 and married. In 1906, he and his family homesteaded in Oklahoma's Cimarron Territory, moved on to coastal Texas ten years later, and returned to the Oklahoma homestead after less than two years. Finally, unpredictable weather and family pride forced the family to leave Oklahoma for Colorado.

This is a geographic story that explains one turn-of-the-century man's struggle—some physical and some social—to make a living for his family. Charley Craft was truly adventuresome and admired by his North Carolina relatives for his charisma, fortitude, and perseverance. His life experiences and concern for his family's future led him on a geographic odyssey in the late 1800s and the first three decades of the 1900s.

He left a hardscrabble farm in North Carolina, worked on farms in Indiana, homesteaded in Oklahoma, worked for a dairy in Texas, returned to the homestead, and finally settled as a truck farmer in Colorado. His is a story of hardship as he and his family weathered the harsh social and physical environments of turn-of-the-century rural North Carolina Piedmont and Oklahoma's Panhandle prairie in the early 20th century. There were, however, hints of a deeper story buried in oral family history. In fact, troubling, unanswered questions persisted for his immediate family throughout the last century, despite repeated efforts by some to find the answers. Only recently did I begin to piece together from oral histories and numerous other sources a family story of epic dimensions and repeated tragedies, some of which were unknown even to the family.

I heard stories about Charley Craft and his family throughout my childhood, but the stories from my father and uncles had little meaning for me. In 1953, however, while on a cross-country trip from North Carolina to Philmont Scout Ranch in New Mexico, I first visited Charley's oldest son, Paul, and his wife, Flossie, in Oklahoma City. Thus began a long-term relationship with the Craft family. I realized that this story about a proud, hardworking family had to be told.

I began researching the Charley Craft family history in earnest in the mid-1980s. It was not until 1988, however, that I began audio-taping interviews with his remaining family members. Over the next 14 years, Harold and Velma Craft graciously invited me into their Wheatridge, Colorado, home to tape hours of in-depth interviews with three of Charley's six children, Harold Craft, Maurie Craft Lang, and Beulah Craft Carpenter Son, as well as Beulah's daughter Jeanne Baker and Harold's wife, Velma. They reminisced at length about their lives and the experiences of living on the Craft homestead between 1905 and 1924 and recounted some of their family's most personal and sometimes painful details.

I also interviewed Wayne Lewis, an 87-year old Gate, Oklahoma, resident, who knew the family in the 1920s and whose help with this story was invaluable. Martha Leinbach, a relative in Winston-Salem, North Carolina, had some documentation about Charley's early life in North Carolina, although much of it was unsubstantiated. Paul Wilburn Jones, a cousin, had visited the Craft family, had heard Charley Craft's North Carolina relatives reminiscing about him, and provided detailed information that assisted in reviving details from my own memory. Steve Lineback, my brother and a civil engineer, provided assistance in locating deeds and genealogy of Charley's North Carolina relations. Charles Robert Craft, Charley Craft's grandson and namesake in Colorado, provided technical information critical to understanding the Craft's land deals in Oklahoma. Others from Charley's family provided photographs, property deeds, and handwritten letters and postcards.

Long-time Gate residents Everett and Ernestine Maphet verified several critical facts about the Craft farm. And 92-year old Randall Carpenter of Boise, Idaho, provided insight into the Crafts' departure from Oklahoma. Special thanks go to all of those who generously assisted in finding the truths involved in the life and times of Charley Craft.

The staff from the Beaver County, Oklahoma, Clerk's Office helped search the county records dating back to Oklahoma's pre-statehood, finding more than 20 critical legal documents. From the lengthy and detailed interviews, family oral history, public records and newspapers, and sometimes through deduction, I pieced together what I believe to be a true-life story of a rural North Carolinian turned Oklahoma homesteader.

Ruth Cook, my former administrative assistant, provided invaluable transcriptions of many hours of almost unintelligible tapes of conversations with Craft family members. Jane Nicholson, Director of University News at Appalachian State University and my long-time professional friend, graciously spent many hours editing and recommending changes to the manuscript. Kathy Brown, Secretary to the Department of Geography and Planning, also provided editorial suggestions.

My sincere appreciation goes to my wife Katie and daughters Mandy and Mitzi for their support over the years.

This manuscript is a labor of love, dedicated to the Charles Vachel Craft family.

Neal G. Lineback

CHAPTER 1

COMING OF AGE IN NORTH CAROLINA

The North Carolina Piedmont Setting

In the late 1800s, North Carolina's rural Piedmont landscape around Forsyth County was composed mostly of 50- to 300-acre farms. Most farmers grew corn and hay to feed cattle, hogs, and chickens and vegetable crops and wheat to feed large farm families. Some also raised cash crops of tobacco to be sold at auction in and around Winston (now Winston-Salem). Small towns, usually named for prominent local families, dotted the landscape about six or seven miles apart. A general store located in each town provided very basic goods and services of the time—hardware, seeds, harness and farm implements, dry goods, groceries, and basic clothing. Folks living in these small towns usually worked as clerks, teachers, ministers, and millers, while the surrounding people lived on and worked their farms.

Except for the loamy, fertile soils of stream floodplains, North Carolina Piedmont soils are heavy clay, subject to compaction, difficult to work with horse-drawn implements, and hard to cultivate or hoe in dry weather. A typical 100-acre farm of Piedmont clay required the work of several "hands" in order for a family to make a modest living. Typically, families of five to eleven children worked together, with the children throughout their childhood and teenage years supplementing the parents' labor. This meant that each large farm family had a ready and growing source of free labor for 15 to 25 years or more, depending upon the number and spacing of their children's ages.

Those farm couples who were barren or who had married late in life and had only one or two children, however, often sought other ways of making a livelihood while continuing to live on the farm. Some of these men worked at other jobs and left the daily farm work up to the wife and children, but others looked for innovative ways to supplement the labor—even raising relatives' children. During planting, harvesting, or other times when considerable labor was required for brief periods, local farmers helped each other. The daily grind of only one or two people operating a 100-acre farm was overpowering. Animals to feed, cows to milk, horses to tend, hoeing and harvesting crops, and fences to mend were more than one person could handle.

Social structures in North Carolina's rural Piedmont in the late 1800s revolved around churches. The social leader tended to be the local preacher, who often helped set and administer levels of social justice based on the general social mores of the day. Churches played valuable roles in birth, marriage, and death, as well as traditional Sunday and holiday worship.

Without daily access to newspapers or radio in the late 1800s, rural communities on the Piedmont were quite isolated. Such isolation led residents to be closely attuned to local issues, particularly dealing with births, marriages, deaths, and community happenings. Few things went on in such communities without full knowledge of the entire population.

Charles Vachel Craft was born into this setting to Junius Irving and Harriet Jane Kimel Craft in Lewisville, North Carolina, on 20 October 1872 **(Fig. 1.1)**.

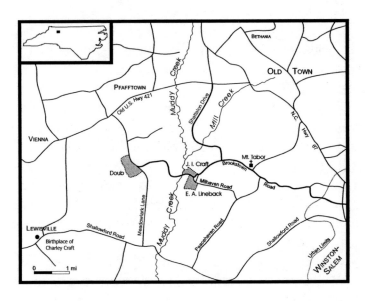

Fig. 1.1. Charley Craft's World, 1872-1890

The Birth of Charles Vachel Craft, Lewisville, North Carolina

Junius Craft, Charley's father, was born on 21 March 1842, in Lewisville, North Carolina He was conscripted into the Confederate Army on 1 July 1862 and served as a private in Company H 33rd Regiment, North Carolina.

Wounded in the ankle at Fredericksburg, Virginia, he was discharged in 1863. Relatively late in life at the age of 29, Junius and Harriet Jane Kimel were married on 21 September 1871, in the home of the bride's grandfather in nearby Winston.[1]

The Craft house at the time was a small log structure about one city block from the center of the small town of Lewisville. Harriet Jane Kimel Craft, a young woman probably less than 20 years old, gave birth to her first and only child, Charles Vachel Craft, on 20 October 1872. It was the custom of the time to give birth at home and, in this case, probably with only the accompaniment of a midwife. Less than two months after giving birth, Harriet Jane died tragically, probably in the same room where her son had been born. Her death was likely from a complication—perhaps an infection—during childbirth, a common malady of the time. Junius was left with baby Charles (or Charley, as he was called), for whom he could not care as a single parent. The baby needed a wet nurse and Junius needed to work.

Junius was a businessman, who co-owned or rented a small general store in nearby Winston, where he traveled daily to work. His partner's surname was Griffin, and they operated a small general store, locally called a "jottum down" store, located on North Trade Street.[2] Junius realized that he could not care for a newborn baby and that he needed a family to care for baby Charley.

As was the custom at the time, Junius sought to place baby Charley in a *bound boy* situation. Junius's sister Theresa Craft Doub agreed to take baby Charley, nurse him for the short term, and raise him as part of her family. Such *bound child* situations were accepted as informal adoptions of the child, who was to be raised as one of the adoptive family's own.

The tradition of placing a child in a *bound* situation dates back before the 1800s in North Carolina, perhaps even to the earliest European settlement. High death rates, particularly of mothers at childbirth, meant that many relatives or non-relatives raised children who weren't their own. Throughout rural America prior to 1900, children were considered assets on farms. Adding another child to a rural family was often seen as a long-term benefit to the family.

Whether the relationship between the *bound child* and the adoptive parent was a blood relationship or not, there was usually some bonding that went on in the family, particularly if the adoptive mother suckled the *bound child* soon after birth. Occasionally, however, economic, health, social, or personal issues could interfere within the intra-family relationship between the *bound child* and the adoptive family. Generally, the adoptive family was expected to treat the *bound child* as a member of the family.

Life as a *Bound Boy* in Pfafftown, North Carolina

Being a *bound boy* or *girl* in rural North Carolina during the latter part of the 19th century carried with it a certain stigma. For example, once the "deal" was made between the biological parent and the adoptive family, whether with a written agreement or not, it was nearly impossible to break. This left the child to be raised however the adoptive family saw fit. Typically, the child's natural parent gave up all claims to the child and the child temporarily lost most legal connections to the biological parent. Once done, the process left little possibility for anything more than a social relationship between the natural parent and the child, if indeed there could be a relationship at all.

In Charley Craft's case, the adoptive parents were Theresa Craft Doub, Junius's sister and Charley's aunt, and her husband, Rev. Daniel Doub, a local Methodist preacher. The Rev. Doub and Theresa were married 24 May 1866, when both were considerably older than most newlyweds of that time. He was 52 and she was 36 years of age. Perhaps because of their ages, the Doubs had only one child, a boy named Boyd. Boyd Vachel Doub was born in 1869, making him three years old when Charley was born. Apparently, Boyd was still being breast-fed by Theresa when Charley came into the family, as breast-feeding often continued well beyond a child's third birthday. Because Boyd was Theresa's first child and, at 39 years of age, she was nearing the end of her childbearing age, she would have had a very close relationship with her own child when Charley came into the family.[3]

One would think that there also would have been a close bond between Theresa and Charley, since she breast-fed him too. It was the impression of Charley's blood relatives, who continued to keep in touch with *bound boy* Charley, however, that his adoptive family, the Doubs, treated him as "a slave." In later years, he was forced to carry out all chores and housework at their bidding, they dressed him poorly, and he was not treated as an equal to the Doubs' son Boyd.[4]

There is more to this portion of Charley Craft's story, however, than these simple descriptions tell. It may have been true that Charley was treated poorly, but there is also circumstantial evidence that he may have been forced by economic circumstances to assume a major role on the Doub farm as a youngster.

Charley was only two years old when Rev. Daniel Doub, his adoptive father, died. His death left Theresa with a farm of several hundred acres to run. Theresa was now 45 years old with two young boys to raise, Boyd at five and Charley at two years of age. The amount of labor necessary to make a living on the 300-acre Doub farm would have been far greater than a woman with two small children could handle.

Theresa probably followed several strategies. She would have received occasional family and neighborly help and would have hired temporary labor to help during planting, harvesting, and fall meat preparation. She also may have allowed tenant farmers and/or sharecroppers to farm the land for rent or for a portion of the income, respectively.

The most help on the farm may have come from a black farmer named Pleas Bailey. It is not clear whether Pleas was a neighboring laborer paid by Theresa to work on the Doub farm, a tenant farmer who lived on the farm, or a sharecropper who farmed part of the Doub farm on shares. It was clear, however, that Pleas Bailey's kindness and work ethic made a lifelong impression on Charley Craft. Charley pronounced Pleas's name, "Plez," as did Charley's children.[5]

Pleas Bailey was part of a rural black community located between Lewisville and nearby Pfafftown on the Lewisville-Vienna Road. The first Bailey family members moved from Walnut Cove in Stokes County, North Carolina, to the community after the Civil War.[6] The Bailey family history is not recorded at all, but it is likely that Pleas was one of the first Baileys to arrive in the Pfafftown area and would have been looking for work.

It is unclear how much time Pleas Bailey spent at the Doub farm, but Charley remembered him fondly in his later years. Charley's experience with this kindly worker and caretaker had a positive effect on his attitude toward minorities. Charley enjoyed hunting and often spoke fondly to his children about his hunting experiences with Pleas Bailey.[7]

Throughout his childhood, however, Charley clearly endured a difficult family life. While many of his extended family believed he was forced into virtual servitude, it may have been out of necessity. Indeed, as he grew into adolescence, Charley may have realized that he had to become more and more responsible for the operation of the Doub farm. The Doub family was likely cash poor, and Charley may have realized that he had some farming abilities essential to operating the farm. Perhaps he also enjoyed the rigor and outdoor nature of farming.

Charley's North Carolina relatives thought that Charley's cousin, Boyd, led a relatively carefree life, often directing Charley to do his bidding on the Doub farm.[8] Given the family's economic circumstances, the death of his stepfather, Rev. Doub, and Charley's penchant for farming, it is not clear whether the hard work was necessary for the family's survival or simply Charley's choice. Since he was a *bound boy*, he may have felt duty-bound to work the farm, or he may have found pleasure in running the

8

farm. Whatever the reason, Charley gained considerable farming experience on the Doub farm as an adolescent and teenager.

Farming the red clay soils of the North Carolina Piedmont was difficult, but Charley perhaps hoped for a future in farming. He may have attended school through a few grades, but he likely arrived at school dressed poorly and unkempt, probably in red clay-stained overalls. He would have milked the cows twice daily from the time he was only six or seven years of age and most likely would have been involved in making butter and cheese on the farm. He would have worked in the fields in the spring, summer, and fall, planting, cultivating, and harvesting by hand and with horses. At about 300 acres, the Doub farm was larger than most nearby farms, but was otherwise typical of Piedmont farms of the day. It would have been about half pastured and the rest planted in corn, wheat, or hay, with a sizeable garden that produced vegetables for canning. Charley grew up knowing hard work, the daily rhythms and rigors of farm life, and the fickleness of farm production. This experience was to play a critical role in the remainder of his life, as he moved on to Indiana, Oklahoma, Texas, and finally to Colorado. It became clear that he was very bright, he understood farming, and he could be successful at it, given the opportunity.

The Junius Craft Family

When Charley was nearly two years old and living with his adoptive Doub family, his natural father, Junius Craft, married his second wife, Martha Styers, on 23 September 1874. Martha Styers came from a wealthy family and met Junius in his little store on Trade Street in

Winston when she and her father came to shop. Within 10 years, the Junius Craft family had built a house on a 500-acre farm given to the couple by Martha's father near the corner of Country Club Road and Peace Haven Road, just west of present-day Winston-Salem.

With the help of their oldest child, Della, Junius and Martha hauled bricks and built their large house on the site. Their other child, Etta, was a baby at the time. Two of their young children, Buelah and Calvin, died in infancy of the flux on this farm. Flux was a common disease among infants of the time and would now be known as dysentery, a bacterial disease that usually came from contaminated water or milk. After these tragic deaths, Martha became despondent. Around 1880, Junius sold the farm and bought the "Pfaff House" and 98-acre farm located on Brookstown Road (now Robin Hood or Robinhood Road) in the Mt. Tabor community of Forsyth County. From the union between Junius and Martha Styers, three more girls and one boy were born (Jenny, Daisy, Blanche, and Sam, respectively), totaling six living children. Junius and Martha lived out their lives in this house, which was to become known as "The Craft House."

Because Charley was no longer part of the Junius Craft family, it is unclear whether he was welcomed into the Craft House by his stepmother, Martha Styers Craft. Although no one remembered Charley ever spending a night in the Craft House, there is circumstantial evidence that he had a positive relationship with his father, Junius. It is very likely that he also visited his halfsister at the Craft house, however, and perhaps he was invited to meals there (**Fig. 1.2**). All of Charley's half-sisters knew of his plight in his bound boy situation, clearly felt sorry for him and dearly loved him as an older halfbrother. He apparently had a winning way with his half-nephews, even though most would not meet him until they were adults. Charley's halfsister Della and Etta passed down oral histories about Charley to their children.[9]

Della, Charley's oldest half-sister, married Ellis Lineback on 16 September 1894 and soon moved into a small two-room house almost diagonally across Brookstown Road from the Junius Craft property.[10] Ellis and Della later built a larger home by salvaging an old log frame-construction millhouse from Mill Creek (just north of Milhaven Road) given to them by Junius. With the millhouse as a core, Ellis built the Lineback house that still stands at the corner of Robinhood and Milhaven roads. The fact that Junius was so generous to Della and Ellis is interesting because there was little evidence that Junius ever provided any support for Charley while he was growing up in the Doub household, a fact that led to considerable speculation later by Charley's children.

Della and Ellis Lineback had eleven children, but all of their children would have been born after Charley left North Carolina. Nonetheless, Della instilled in all of her children a love for her halfbrother Charley by telling them stories about him. Freda, born 24 June 1895, and Eula, born 30 January 1897, would remember Charley fondly, although they never met him until years later. There is no denying a special relationship between Charley and Della.

As a teenager, Charley was particularly isolated in the Pfafftown society, where he and his adoptive family lived. Everyone knew Charley's bound boy history, knew that he might have no legal inheritance from the Doubs, and knew that the Doub family would hold him in servitude as long as possible. His standing in the Pfafftown, Lewisville, and Mt. Tabor communities left his future in considerable doubt despite his jovial and likeable personality.[11]

Fig. 1.2. The Junius Craft House, formerly the James Pfaff House, circa 1978. The house was removed professionally from the site on Robin Hood Road in 2001 by Chris Buckles and reconstructed on property in Advance in Davie County, NC. Note the attached kitchen on the right, which was added by Junius to the original house *(Photograph taken by Hershel "Hank" Tyson and permission granted by Doris Tyson [2005])*

Not unlike rural communities throughout the country at the end of the 19th century, those on the North Carolina Piedmont were tight-knit. Outsiders were accepted cautiously, everyone knew everything about everyone else, and suitors still asked for the hands of their brides-to-be. Communities were mostly Methodist, Baptist, or Moravian, and churches were a dominant social force in the lives of the local population, maintaining religious customs and social mores. Deviations from those mores were dealt with in each community by unofficial excommunication, if not from the church, then from society. People would turn their backs, refuse to socialize with the offender, and generally deny him or her a social or economic future in the community.

Throughout his teenage years, Charley lived as a second-class citizen in the Pfafftown society. It is doubtful that, as Charley came of age, he was able to visit the homes of most local girls. He was not able to dress as well as his peers, for his adoptive family provided little for him other than room and board, although he more than paid for his upkeep through his chores and farm work. Without money of his own and appropriate clothing, few of the parents of girls in the community likely welcomed Charley into their homes. His prospects as a husband were poor, indeed, as he had few opportunities and little standing in the local rural community.

Life as a Young Adult in Pfafftown

In late summer of 1889 at the age of only 17, Charley joined some local boys, including Bill Leinbach, to travel by train to Noblesville, Indiana. Bill was Ellis Lineback's brother and husband-to-be of Charley's half-sister Etta. Bill was Charley's contemporary, having also been born in 1872 (4 July). (Ellis changed his surname to an Anglicized spelling of Lineback around 1900 when he successfully ran for a local public office as County Road Commissioner.)

The purpose of Charley's and Bill's trip was to seek paid jobs for farm work in Indiana. Such opportunities were sorely lacking around Piedmont North Carolina in 1889. For several years, a group of young men, including some of those in the Shields family, had traveled annually from the Mt. Tabor community to Indiana to work in the wheat and cornfields. They came back with real cash and stories about their adventures that must have been very enticing to two 17 year olds. The Shields men apparently helped network with Bill Leinbach and Charley to get them work in Indiana.

In fact, at least one of the Shields—Sherman Shields—settled in Carmel, Indiana. At Sherman's home, years later on 18 August 1914, Bill Leinbach died the very night he arrived to work once more in Indiana's fields. The Ellis Lineback family always believed that Bill died of rabies, as he was bitten by a dog thought to be rabid a short time before he left North Carolina on a train trip to Indiana. A Dr. Hershey, who signed his death certificate in Indiana, described his cause of death as uncertain, but perhaps a heart attack.[12] One of the Shields, however, told Ellis that, "Bill went to bed with a severe headache and the bedclothes were torn up [disheveled] when we found him the next morning."[13] Circumstantial evidence suggests that rabies was more probable, particularly since no heart disease appears in the Leinbach/Lineback family.

Charley must have been enticed by the promise of cash for working in Indiana, something he never had much of as he labored on the Doub farm. On the other hand, he had the farming skills, a strong desire to make something of himself, and the need to build a future. At the time he left North Carolina, he still might have thought that his long-term future was in Forsyth County. When he returned to Pfafftown from Indiana after his first year of work, he purchased 12 acres of land from the Doubs for $42.00 along Reynolds Creek in January 1890. In the last year of her life (d. 3 October 1890), Theresa had turned the Doub farm over to her son Boyd. The 12 acres that Charley purchased were located just south of Brookstown Road and about four miles west of Muddy Creek. Charley bought the parcel, called the Doub 12, from Boyd Doub, his cousin.[14]

The exact transaction whereby Charley bought the land is not clear. The fact that he had to pay for the Doub property—albeit, a low price even for that time—might be evidence that Theresa and Boyd did not consider him legally part of the Doub family. On the other hand, since Charley paid so little for the land, he may have been paying only a surveying and/or transfer fee. Boyd and his mother Theresa might have been providing Charley with some sort of grubstake.[15]

Charley's purchase in 1890 of the Doub 12 may have been an attempt on his part to settle into the Pfafftown community, to put down some roots, and to farm there. Sometime following the summer of 1890, however, Charley decided to go back to Indiana to work again, probably with Bill Leinbach—this time to Carmel. Neither of them had married at this time, and their first trip had proven to be profitable. Charley chose to stay in Indiana this time after the harvest season, rather than return to North Carolina. By then, the crops were gathered and there was work available on a dairy farm near Carmel.

It was unclear to Charley's children later in life as to why Charley decided to leave Pfafftown. Some thought it was the community's unwillingness to accept him because of his bound boy status. Others thought that Charley had greater aspirations and that he had seen an opportunity in Indiana when he worked there initially. There was even some suspicion that he had met his future bride, Martha, while working. This remained a mystery for his friends and many of Charley's family. In 1988, eldest daughter Buelah Craft Son described her memories of why Charley left North Carolina:

> *Papa [Charley] went to Indiana at the same times as ... Bill [Leinbach]. They got a job working there. Jobs were few and far between. Papa worked on a dairy farm. One of the reasons he went from North Carolina to Indiana was that he had two aunts [in North Carolina]. But, anyway, they got tired of managing him. When there was a wagonload of people going to Indiana, they sent Papa. At that time he was a grown man. Of course, there was nothing--North Carolina was still suffering from the war [Civil War]. It was good to move away from there. And nothing for a young man in wages for anything [in North Carolina].*

In fact, years later, in the 1960s, according to Buelah, Charley's daughter Maurie returned to North Carolina, searching courthouse records, seeking answers to questions about why Charley left.[16]

Charley's departure from North Carolina may have perplexed his children later in life, but to his North Carolina relatives, his reason for departing for Indiana for the second and final time was no secret.

Charley's Secret

Charley Craft left North Carolina under considerable personal duress. The reasons he left, however, involved a secret about his youth that was kept from his immediate family for more than 100 years.

In fact, through three generations, the North Carolina Crafts and Leinbachs/Linebacks had an unwritten pact not to divulge Charley's secret to any of his immediate family. Keeping the secret just seemed to Charley's North Carolina relatives to be the right thing to do. Charley's descendents were very proud, and there was concern that revealing his secret would be a major embarrassment to them. This information just would have been too painful for Charley and Martha's children, even though the children themselves made at least one trip to North Carolina exclusively in search of the answers. In fact, it is doubtful that Charley ever told his secret to his wife, Martha.[17]

Charley had little social standing in the Pfafftown and Lewisville communities where he was raised by his Aunt Theresa, with the occasional help of two other aunts, Senia and Cynthia. By the time he was 15 years old, there was a Pfafftown girl, Ellen George, who began paying attention to Charley, although she was only 13. This was likely Charley's first romantic involvement.

Ellen George (b. 1873) was the older sister of Cora George (b. 1879), who later married Thomas Henry Hicks. Both Cora and Ellen were illegitimate children of Salina George, who never married and raised both daughters by herself, working as a domestic.[18] She and her two daughters lived in a log cabin just north of the junction of present-day Robinhood Road and old U.S. Highway 421 approximately three miles from the Doub farm.[19] Because of the illegitimacy of her two daughters, Salina George's family probably had a relatively low social standing in the Pfafftown community.

17

On 20 August 1887 at age 14, Ellen George gave birth to a baby. The circumstantial evidence is very strong that Charley Craft was the father of the baby. Oft-repeated Craft and Leinbach/Lineback oral family history confirmed that Charley had fathered a child out of wedlock. The North Carolina relatives believed that the child was one of the Hicks children. This was a misunderstanding, however, connected to the child's caretaker, Cora George, later to become Cora George Hicks.

Perhaps to link the baby to the Craft family, Ellen named the boy Junius Levita George. The name Junius was relatively uncommon outside of the Craft and Leinbach/Lineback families in Forsyth County at that time, with Charley's father, Junius I. Craft, being the only local person carrying that given name.

It is unclear why Charley did not claim the child. Possibly, he might have been unsure whether he was the father. Given Salina George's reputation in the neighborhood, there would have been some question about promiscuity within the family. It is also possible that Charley's relatives advised against his marriage because of the age of both the mother (14) and father (15), although such underage marriages did occur occasionally under such circumstances. Regardless, at that age and under his bound boy status, it would have been clear that Charley could not support a family.

The Crafts, Leinbachs/Linebacks, and the entire community believed that Charley had fathered an illegitimate child named Hicks. The reason for this misunderstanding arose from the fact that Cora George, Ellen's younger sister, largely raised Junius herself in Salina George's house. Cora married Thomas Hicks in

1904 when she was 25 years old. Because she was the younger of the two George girls, she apparently took care of Junius before her marriage while Ellen and Salina worked outside the home. When Cora married Thomas Henry Hicks, Junius would have been 17. This close connection between Cora and her nephew Junius would likely have led the community and Charley's relatives to believe that Junius George was Cora's child, thus the confusion with the Hicks name. It would have been impossible for Junius to be Cora's child, however, as Cora would have only been eight years old when Junius was born. Thus the link with the Hicks family name likely came from confusion about Cora George Hicks's role in Junius's life.

If this speculation about Junius being Charley Craft's child is true, then this helps explain how Charley's reputation in the Pfafftown, Lewisville, and Mt. Tabor communities left him with few social opportunities. Fathering an illegitimate child would have likely sealed his fate.

Charley came back to North Carolina from a season of working in wheat and corn in Indiana to claim the Doub 12 in 1890, and his family and this author conjecture that he had hoped to farm that land permanently. It soon became clear to him that even in the intervening three years, his reputation had not improved, so he left the state for good.

Thus the conclusion is that Charley Craft was pushed out of his North Carolina community by social pressures and that this experience impacted the remainder of his life.

CHAPTER 2

MAKING A LIVING IN INDIANA

Life in Carmel, Indiana, 1891-1904

Charley obtained work on an Indiana dairy farm near Carmel, Indiana, just north of the city of Indianapolis. While there, he met Martha Ann Newby, the daughter of Gideon and Rebecca Florina Harold Newby. Although her memory was fading in her later years, daughter Buelah remembered her mother talking about family members coming to Indiana from North Carolina, particularly her uncle for whom her brother Harold was named.[20]

According to a Newby family record, Gideon (b. 18 March 1830, d. 6 February 1908) and Rebecca (b. 26 June 1835, d. 16 December 1902) were married on 3 March 1865. Apparently, Rebecca had had a previous child, Flavia V. Harold (b. 16 April 1857), born perhaps out of wedlock eight years before she and Gideon married. She and Gideon had five children: Emma (b. 4 January 1866), Lewis B. (b. 16 August 1867), Lenna Leona (b. 24 July 1871), Rachel Ellen (b. 9 September 1873), and Martha Ann (b. 4 August 1876).

Gideon worked at several jobs and from all accounts made a reasonably good living for his family, allowing them to live in the town of Carmel.[21] Martha's mother, Rebecca, called Bella by the family, was a rather large and stern-looking woman, but she and Martha were close **(Fig. 2.1 and 2.2)**. The Newby family lived across the street from a school that Martha attended and where she occasionally helped clean blackboards.

Fig. 2.1 A tintype of Martha Craft's mother, Rebecca Florina Newby, probably taken in Indianapolis, Indiana, circa 1882. She would have been about 47 years old. *(Source: Permission by Velma Craft.)*

Fig. 2.2. A tintype of Martha Newby (Craft) at about age 6, probably taken in Indianapolis, Indiana, circa 1882. *(Source: Maurie Craft Lang's family collection, permission by son Martin Lang.)*

Martha was an attractive young woman, thin and small in stature, and wore her hair in a bun, as was the custom of the day. She was a spirited and energetic individual, as evidenced throughout her life by her willingness to take on new challenges, endure hardships, and battle the elements as a farmwife. She was well educated and able to write articulately. She was also accustomed to the good life in a small Midwest town when she met Charley Craft.

The Newby family was Quaker, attending meetings and worshiping regularly. Gideon was extremely strict, forbidding Martha from participating in anything associated with music. Nonetheless, Martha's mother helped her secretly learn the organ at the school across the street. During a conversation between Maurie Craft Lang and Velma Craft in 1988, Maurie said:

> *In the Quaker religion in Carmel, Indiana, Martha's father felt there shouldn't be a piano or an organ or any musical instrument in church. He felt that singing words had no meaning and that it would be a "lie." But Mom [Martha] did not go along with her father's plan, of course, just like teenagers today. The family lived across the street from the school, where Mom would clean the erasers and help the teacher [in order] to get free organ lessons. But her dad wouldn't let her mother or her have a musical instrument in the house. Zola, Mom's niece, told me five or six times that Mom's Dad [Gideon] was a stinker. If he ever caught Mom playing the piano and singing that he would beat her.*

Ultimately, Martha's father found out about her music lessons at the school and reportedly whipped or beat her. Martha was perhaps only 14 years of age, a young woman at that time. There is circumstantial evidence that Martha never fully forgave her father for the whippings. Even though there were opportunities years later for her to visit her family in Indiana, she went back only once in 1909—a year after her father's death (6 February 1908), probably to help settle his estate. There also is the question of whether the conflict between daughter and father led to Martha's early marriage to Charley Craft and their subsequent departure from Indiana to homestead in Oklahoma.

Just after Christmas 1894 and nearly a year before he married Martha, Charley wrote a letter from Carmel to his North Carolina family (verbatim):

> *Dear ones at home. I would like to see you, But, I can not, so I will now rite you a few lines to let you no that I am well and hop you are the same. I have had a good Chrismas and hope you have had the same. I went to see my girl and had dinner with her. We had a good time and a good dine. The folks that I live with went of[f] on a trip for to weeks. I milk ten cows for to weeks and all the other work. But they treat me mity good. I got a nice Chrismas present of the tree [unintelligible] It was nice last night. It snowed and is cold today. The folks out hear is all well. I have . . . a heap of hard work out here, but I like this place the best of anywhere I ever saw. . . but anywhere else only out here. For I think that I . . . better than anywhere that I saw. I want you to rite and tell me how you are getin along and how Dela is getin along. I would like to see her house and how she is getin a long. I guess that Bill [Leinbach] told you about those pictures that I sent*

*out there. I will lease [not buy a house or land] for
the time. [Write] Soon and let me no how you are
getin a long. Your Son, Charley Craft.[22]*

On 13 November 1895 at the age of 19, Martha
Ann Newby married Charles Vachel Craft, age 23. Charley
had been in Indiana just over four years.

Following their marriage, Charley and Martha
lived for nine years in Carmel, while Charley continued
to work on the dairy farm. They may have been paying
rent or perhaps living on the farm where he worked. During
their first nine years of marriage, Martha gave birth at least
twice.

Their first child, Paul Vachel Craft, was born
on 9 July 1896. Vachel was a Craft family name dating
back to Charley's grandfather, Vachel Craft, born in 1804
in Lewisville, North Carolina. There is evidence in a
family bible that Martha had at least one other child who
did not live very long while the Crafts lived in Carmel.
Lending circumstantial evidence to one or more possible
intervening pregnancies, their second child, Buelah, was
born on 18 December 1902, more than six years after
Paul. In the early 1900s, it was infrequent that a married
woman of childbearing age would go six years without a
pregnancy.[23]

Martha's mother, Rebecca, died on 16 December
1902. It is doubtful that Martha, Charley, and their six-
year-old son, Paul, were living with Gideon and Rebecca at
the time of Rebecca's death, but certainly, her death freed
Martha to leave Carmel. Martha was close to her mother,
and the rift between her and her father may have widened
following her mother's death.

26

This was probably a difficult period, between 1895 and 1903, for the Craft couple as they struggled to make ends meet and to contemplate their young family's future. By 1902, they were desperately searching for opportunities. It was this search that led to their interest in "homesteading" in a Quaker settlement in Oklahoma's Cimarron Territory.

This land in the Oklahoma Panhandle was just opening for homesteading in 1903, and Quakers from around Carmel learned about it from a leading charismatic Quaker educator, Henry Fellow. He was living in Alva, Oklahoma, and had recently purchased some land there on which to build a Friends' Meeting House.[24] He had Quaker connections in Indiana and Kansas, and he solicited money and settlers from his fellow Quakers. Fellow came to Carmel in 1903 and networked within the Quaker community. Charley and Martha, no doubt, listened excitedly as he described the opportunities for assisting in building the religious building in Alva, while seeking free land through homesteading in the nearby Panhandle.

Fellow was a highly educated and energetic Quaker who used every opportunity to recruit members to the faith, to build Quaker meeting houses and educational institutions, and to congregate Quakers in settlements in Kansas and Oklahoma. Very early in his educational career, Fellow demonstrated his money-raising abilities.[25]

It is not clear exactly what else was promised to Charley and Martha for following Henry Fellow to Alva other than the opportunities to work on the church building and to file for a homestead. It is likely that Fellow offered to pay something for their labor and perhaps to provide temporary housing. Of course, he would have offered to help

them find a homestead, but there would have been a great
deal of uncertainty in the specifics. All the young Crafts
had to go on was Fellow's word and his enthusiasm.

Alva, Oklahoma, was Henry Fellow's staging area
for increasing the Quaker population and influence in the
West. Fellow clearly saw the new Quaker frontier as the
Cimarron Territory and realized that Alva with its railroad
head could serve as a jumping-off place for homesteaders.
Fellow's memoirs describe his attempt to move Quakers
into the Oklahoma Panhandle:

> *Alva being the county seat of Old Woods County
> with its great educational Institute [Northwestern
> State Normal School] at hand, this point was
> viewed by Christian workers as a strategic point for
> religious activity. Friends were not slow to take up
> the call pointing westward toward the great Beaver
> County Panhandle and the possible work in S.E.
> Colorado.*

Such an opportunity to follow the well known and
respected Quaker leader to Oklahoma and the promise of
free land to be homesteaded must have seemed fortuitous
to the young Craft couple. Virtually all of Indiana's arable
land was in farms by 1900, and the price was out of the
reach of young farm families. Few could afford to purchase
expensive farmland, a process having been repeated across
the East and Midwest throughout the 1800s. This insatiable
demand for affordable land by the children of large
traditional farm families made free land for homesteaders
seem incredibly attractive, contributing to the westward
migration.

28

The prevalence of large farm families and a rapidly increasing population put heavy pressure on the price of farmland, leaving those without inheritances little opportunity to buy their own farms. Neither Charley nor Martha had inheritances, and they had to rely upon Charley's meager salary as a farm worker in Carmel. Although his income was enough for a single person living in a boarding house, as he and Bill Leinbach had done in the past, it would have been inadequate to both provide for a young and growing family and to buy expensive land.

In the summer of 1904, the Craft family left Indiana for Oklahoma.

Moving to Oklahoma, 1904

Charley and Martha and their two children left Indiana for Oklahoma in the late summer of 1904. Accompanying them were the two other families from Carmel, the John Cards and the Max Smiths, all young and all Quakers. Networking among such Quaker homesteaders encouraged other Quakers from Iowa to join the migration to Oklahoma over the next 15 to 20 years.

Wayne Lewis, long-time resident Quaker of Beaver County described (2002) the process that brought Quakers to the county:

> *Quakers congregated. A bunch of people from the old community came together. So neighbors there were neighbors here [networking]. Except one bunch from each Indiana and Iowa came. Bunch came earlier from Northern Kansas. My father came from Iowa [1915]. They were farmers. And*

there was no more land available [in Iowa]. The ones that got the [family] land [older children] financed the younger ones to come out here and get their own start.

Fellow's memoirs are even more specific:

The first Quakers to settle in Gate Valley were the Kerseys and Moons from Iowa and the Parkers and Knowles came likewise and settled west of the Harrises, near the village of Knowles some ten miles west of Gate. Dr. Dugan (sic) of North Carolina Quaker heritage had lived here many years and was the community doctor.

The Crafts might have saved some small amount of money from Charley's salary, but the growing family needed more. On 27 October 1902, two months before the birth of their second child, Buelah, both Charley and Martha deeded the Doub 12 in North Carolina to Charley's father, Junius. The transaction took place in Indiana, and the deed was sent to Junius in North Carolina. The intent of the transaction was to have Junius sell the property for Charley and Martha.[26]

Whether Junius advanced them some money is unknown, but he was unable to sell the property until two years later. Even then, Junius had to hold a note on the property for several years in order to receive full payment.[27]

If Junius advanced Charley some money before he sold the Doub 12 to William Parks, that could have added to the pool of money necessary to finance the trip to Oklahoma. Junius may have just sold the Doub 12 about the time of Charley and Martha's departure to Oklahoma in the summer of 1904. Charley and Martha were probably desperate to receive the money for their land.

Perhaps contributions from Martha's family members in Indiana may have also helped the Crafts. Martha's aunt's family, the Frosts, exhibited a long and lasting relationship with the Crafts in general and with Paul, the oldest son, in particular. In addition, the Quakers in Carmel and elsewhere through Henry Fellow's efforts may have contributed to the cost of the move.

The Craft family chartered a railcar with John Card's and Max Smith's families to move all of their household goods. Alva, the railhead for western Oklahoma, is located 73 miles due east of Gate.[28]

Son Harold Craft (1996) remembered Charley's friend John Card, whose family was one of those who accompanied Charley's family from Indiana:

> *Accompanying them was another man, John Card and his family, who became lifelong friends with the Craft family. John, who was a carpenter by trade, told friends and neighbors that he would follow Charley anywhere.*

Their likely arrival in the summer (or perhaps early fall) of 1904 is substantiated by several sources. The timing allowed Charley to find a homestead, arrange to file and settle on it, and to be ready to farm it.

Paul would have been eight years old, and Buelah was old enough to be "pulling up" (although she would have been about eighteen months old). Buelah (1988) described what she remembered about the family's arrival in Beaver County:

> When the folks moved out there from Indiana, they took a train to Alva, Oklahoma, and [later?] a covered wagon from Alva to Gate. I was so young [when we arrived in Oklahoma] I couldn't walk, but could pull myself up. Mom always would laugh and make a joke out of [my efforts to walk].

Perhaps because they arrived in Alva toward the end of the growing season in 1904, the Crafts, Cards, and Smiths were recruited to help Henry Fellow and other Quakers build the place of worship. Fellow's memoirs said:

> It became apparent that a permanent [Quaker] church home was necessary, so lots were purchased in the middle of the block west of Montforts [?] Bookstore [in Alva], and the money was raised for the building. . . . The foundation was laid and we were ready to place the corner stone when, lo, three families from Hoosierdom landed in Alva and appeared upon the scene. John and Rilla Card, Max and May Smith, and Charles and Mattie Craft—all of whom were carpenters—came at the appointed time and built our church building.

The Crafts spent the fall of 1904 building the Quaker church in Alva. No doubt, Henry Fellow paid them for their work through contributions he had collected. This time in Alva perhaps gave them an opportunity to assess the homesteading potential of lands inside the eastern edge of the Cimarron Territory.[29]

32

In 1905, Henry Fellow claimed a relinquishment as a homestead for himself just inside the Cimarron Territory to the east of the small settlement of Gate. A relinquishment was land that had been filed on by a previous homesteader, who then either abandoned the land or contracted with a realtor to sell his interest in the land. The cost of filing on a homestead initially was $1.25 per acre, but the cost of taking over a relinquishment could have been more. [30]

Homesteaders in the Panhandle were required to file on their property with the U.S. Land Office in Woodward, Oklahoma, located about 45 miles southeast of Gate. Upon filing, the claimant had to be at least 18 years old or married and own no other land and had to live on the property at least six months out of the year for six years, plow part of the acreage, and improve the place with buildings and fences. At the end of six years, the claimant would have "proved up" their claim by having it inspected and, assuming all requirements were met, a patent would be granted, officially deeding the land to the claimant.

As soon as Henry Fellow filed on his property in Gate in the fall of 1904, Max Smith, John Card, and Charley Craft left their wives and children behind in Alva and proceeded to build a soddy[31] on Fellow's property and assist in building the Laurence Friends Academy **(Figs. 2.3 and 2.4)**. Fellow's soddy may have been planned as a "staging house" for the new homesteaders to use for a few months while they were filing on and improving their own homesteads the following spring. Henry and Melissa Fellow sponsored the construction of the Academy as the only accredited high school around Gate. With Henry Fellow leading the way to Gate, Oklahoma, the Crafts and the other three families followed.[32]

In February 1905, the Crafts, Cards, and Smiths took their children out of school in Alva, bought horses and covered wagons in Alva, and moved their households 73 miles westward to Gate. May Smith and her children (and perhaps the other women and children too) took a train to Englewood, Kansas, north of Gate where they were met on a cold February day for the 15-mile trip by wagon to Gate.[33]

Fig. 2.3. Laying the foundation of the first building of the Laurence Friends Academy in Gate, Oklahoma, 1905. *(Source: Maurie Craft Lang's family collection, permission by son Martin Lang.)*

Fig. 2.4. With the Administration building completed (left), the second building is underway to complete the campus of Laurence Friends Academy, Gate, Oklahoma, circa 1906. *(Source: Maurie Craft Lang's family collection, permission by son Martin Lang.)*

The trip was an adventure for the children and parents alike and would have taken two days as they came by train from Alva to Englewood then by wagon to Gate. Had they come from Alva to Gate by wagon, the trip would have taken two or three days to cover the 73 miles, but it would have been a much harder trip on all of them in the middle of the winter. Wagons were essential, as they could provide sleeping quarters, at least for the men, during the first months on each of the homesteads as the families built houses and outbuildings, dug wells, and broke ground for crops. This was truly the Wild West for the Crafts, who had been living in the "lap of luxury" in comparison.

Maurie Craft Lang, in a conversation with Harold Craft (1995), questioned the status of the Panhandle:

Because it [Oklahoma Panhandle] hadn't been deeded to Oklahoma, it was still in question between the Indians and the Oklahoma state, or what?

Harold replied:

> *It just happened to be a strip of ground that wasn't in Oklahoma or Texas or Colorado or Kansas, either one. It was not in any of the Indian Territory or in the Cherokee Strip. That's right. It was just a Panhandle for which amounted to three counties.*

In 1998, Harold had described what he knew or had heard about the situation at the time the Crafts settled on their homestead:

> *This No-Man's Land was known as the Cimarron Territory. When this creek [Horse Creek] was settled by homesteaders from 1902 to 1904, there was considerable friction between the cattlemen and the settlers. A free-range law was in force at that time. Under this law it was necessary for a settler to have a legal fence around his field before he could [claim] any damage to his crops by range cattle. A legal fence was defined as having not less than three well-stretched wires with posts not less than a rod [16.5 feet] apart and two stays between posts.*

Buelah (1988), being older than Harold, actually remembered Gate before the railroad came and added:

> *Well, there is a little truth to the whole thing. They drove cattle from Texas to Englewood, Oklahoma, because it was the end of the rail line. We didn't have any rail in Gate at that time.*

CHAPTER 3

SEEKING A HOMESTEAD IN OKLAHOMA

The Craft Family's Homestead

The Crafts arrived in Oklahoma in 1904 and homesteaded in Gate in the Spring of 1905. Charley filed for a relinquishment on 120 acres, or three adjacent quarter-quarter sections of 40 acres each. The legal description of the farm's location was the N ½ of the SW ¼ and the NW ¼ of the SE ¼ of Sec.15, T5 N, R28E, making up three quarter-quarter sections. The southwest corner of the farm was located on the north side of a broad draw, or gulch, only a mile from Old Gate, the original site of the town of Gate **(Fig. 3.1).** The farm that Charley settled on was a relinquishment of only 120 acres rather than the normal 160 acres of most homesteads.

Five years later, on 8 August 1910, Charley applied for a Final Receipt Record, called a Certificate and the document was recorded on 25 August 1910. This meant that he had paid in full all filing fees, fulfilled all requirements, and applied for a patent (of ownership) on the homestead. Charley then executed his patent on his homestead on 6 March 1911, but it was not officially recorded for some reason until 26 October 1914. When he finally received his patent, this finalized the process and Charley and his family officially owned their homestead.

The homesteading processes were not always the same, particularly if a squatter already occupied the land or if relinquishment were involved. Ernestine Maphet, local resident and author, states,[34]

Sometimes the homesteader would buy out a squatter's rights and file on it. A team of oxen was traded for a quarter [of a section] of ground, horses or mules were traded and some paid a small amount of money for the place. This often saved man troubles between the squatter and the homesteader. A homesteader had to "stake" his claim and travel to Woodward, the nearest filing office to obtain his patent.

Many families stayed a year or two, found life too difficult for whatever reasons, and simply walked away from the land. In such cases, the land became available once more as a relinquishment for homesteading. The next homesteader would claim the land as a relinquishment, register it at Woodward, and begin his or her occupation of the land. And the clock would begin ticking again.[35]

How the Craft farm came to be 120 acres rather than the normal quarter section of 160 acres is not clear, but the facts lend considerable credence to the probability that someone else had claimed it earlier. For example, almost all of the land around Gate was officially rangeland prior to 1898, but squatters and ranchers claimed portions and, in fact, often were in conflict over the same parcel of land. Sometimes two squatters even claimed the same piece, even though there was no legality to any of the claims beyond the claimant's ability to protect his or her own claim—often with guns.[36]

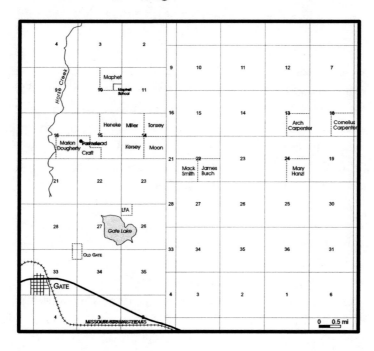

Fig. 3.1. The Craft Homestead and Environs, Gate, Oklahoma, 1905-1924

Therefore, it was into this mix of previous land claims and ownerships that the homesteaders came in 1904 and 1905. Ranchers and squatters used or claimed almost all of the land at one time or another, but up until 1890, they had no legal claim to it. Local Ernestine Maphet in *Gate to No Man's Land* described the origin of the Panhandle:

> *In 1890 the Organic Act provided that "No Man's Land" together with other lands west of the Five*

Civilized Tribes, except the Cherokee Outlet
should be added to the opened territory. At the
same time it provided for setting up a government
and laws for Oklahoma Territory divided into
seven counties. No Man's Land [the Panhandle]
was the seventh county.

The Craft farm was a hardscrabble farm, smaller than most others around and seemingly with poorer potential. For one thing, the farm was located mostly on a south-facing slope of a broad east-west draw, exposed to both the summer sun and drying south wind. Only on occasion was there water in the otherwise dry stream bed.

During wet years, the draw through the Craft farm drained Gate Lake, a shallow, intermittent lake located to the southeast of the farm. To the northeast of Gate Lake was another, even shallower depression called Dishpan Lake. These are natural lakes formed, probably as a result of the solution of limestone 100 to 150 feet below the surface, producing in some mild subsidence at the surface.[37]

During the occasional year that Gate Lake overflowed its natural depression, it provided running water to the normally dry draw that crossed the Craft farm. Such years would have been wetter than normal and probably productive crop years as well. Since this source of water was so intermittent, it was considered not to be a dependable source of water for irrigation on the Craft farm.

During heavy, flashy spring or summer thunderstorms, water would drain through the normally dry streambed on the Craft farm toward the west, where it joined Horse Creek, which in turn flowed to the Cimarron

River to the north. Such rapid runoff was probably seen more as a problem than as a resource by the Crafts, as it would have damaged any crops in the bottom of the draw.

The soils of the Craft farm were typical of those in nearby sections, but because of the draw and somewhat steeper topography than the surrounding homesteads, erosion appears to have been prevalent on the Craft land. In fact, slopes of 3 to 5 percent occurred on both sides of the draw, while sections to the east of the Craft property appear to have much less steepness and relief. The USDA Soil Survey Series (1959, No. 11) describes the soils on and around the Craft homestead as:

> *Mansic soils, severely eroded. Shallow, highly calcareous soils with about half of the subsoil exposed. Developed on uplands from medium-textured and hard caliche materials.*

In several places on the steeper parts of the east-west draw on the Craft farm and around the sites of the barn and house, there is evidence that the topsoil has eroded. Because of the slope, the soil tends to be thin. This is attributed to past cultivation, cattle grazing, and occasional flash floods that removed exposed and loosened soil particles. Where the topsoil has been lost entirely, *caliche*, a white, crusty deposit of calcareous material, is exposed to the surface. *Caliche* typically occurs beneath soils in warm semiarid or desert regions around the world. This condition of having *caliche* exposed at the surface is not unique to the Craft farm and appears commonly on moderate slopes throughout Beaver County.[38]

Consequently, the Craft farm was described by long-time Gate resident Everett Maphet as[39]:

41

. . . a real poor farm, as it was small and had little good farmland.

This description of the farm belies the fact that in good years, the Crafts could make a living on it. Some years, however, brought poor harvests everywhere. According to Harold Craft (1985), Charley also rented nearby land as a way to increase the land under his control and to increase his family income.

On 6 March 1911, six years after filing, Charley received his patent, which meant that he had received ownership of his land. The patent read:

> *To All to Whom these presents shall come—Greeting: Whereas, a certificate of the Register of the Land Office at Woodward, Oklahoma, has been deposited in the General Land Office, whereby it appears that pursuant to the Act of Congress of May 20, 1862, "To Secure Homesteads to Actual Settlers on the Public Domain," and the acts supplemental thereto, the claim of Charles V. Craft has been established and duly consummated, in conformity to law, for the North half of the Southwest Quarter and the Northwest Quarter of the Southeast quarter of Section fifteen in Township five North of Range twenty-eight East of the Cimarron Meridian, Oklahoma, containing one hundred and twenty acres.*[40]

Life in Gate, Oklahoma, 1905-1912

Gate, Oklahoma, is located 73 miles west of Alva, about three miles north of the Beaver River and five miles

42

south of the Cimarron River. At the eastern end of the Panhandle, Gate was one of many early settlements in what was to become Beaver County.

It must have been an exhilarating, if daunting, sight to the young Craft family. They arrived on this nearly treeless prairie with a team of horses and a wagon filled with all of their life's possessions. Since it was still winter when they arrived in February 1905, the Crafts had to share Henry and Melissa Fellow's soddy for a few months until Charley and John Card could dig a well and build a house on the Craft homestead. Henry Fellow's memoirs describe the Crafts' efforts to occupy their homestead:

> *Melissa [Mrs. Fellows] lived in one end of our little 12 X 24 house, using 8 X 12, while Charley and Mattie Craft and kids [Paul and Buelah] occupied the other part. He broke out the farm and raised the first crop and a little stock.*

Charley and John Card lived out of the wagon that spring, while Charley dug a well and he and John Card constructed a bank house or partial dugout (not a soddy). The house was about half beneath ground in a trench, of sorts, but the frame and roof were constructed of wood. Through the spring and summer, they completed the house and worked during the fall to build a trench barn, similar to the bank house. Buelah (1988) remembered:

> *John Card was the so-called carpenter. That's one of the first things was to drill [dig] a well. Now I don't know if Max Smith [who came to Gate with Charley's and John Card's families] built his house first or not. I know some of them lived in [our] dugout while they were building it. Max Smith and*

May [his wife]--I slept at the foot of their bed [in their house]--because they had no other bed for me to sleep in. [We] were trying to make room for Pop and Mom [Charley and Martha]. I don't know where they slept. I don't remember that the folks stayed with them [the Smiths] because I think they were over at the area where our well was being put in.

The lumber used to construct the dugout probably came from eastern Oklahoma or Arkansas, brought by rail to the railhead at Englewood, Kansas. It would have traveled the rest of the way to Gate by wagon. Harold (1996) didn't know where the Crafts bought the wood to build their house and barn:

There was a lumber company in Gate, surely. Whether there was one there at that time [in the early years], I don't know. But I know there was one in Englewood, Kansas. It was across the Cimarron River into Kansas.

Englewood was about 15 miles due north and the likely source of lumber was there, but it required crossing the Cimarron River. This stream could be "flashy" during summer thunderstorms when intense local rainfall caused a quick rise in floodwater. Occasionally, it would be high during spring thaws. Other Gate residents did not remember it being a particular problem, but Maurie Craft Lang and Harold Craft remembered its dangers well.[41]

The Craft's farm was 120 acres, although Harold remembered (1995) that it had 160, which would have made it a full quarter section:

Besides the 160 acres, or a quarter section, my dad always leased more ground around. And just how much I don't know. I just remember going with him on the hayrack and getting fodder from other places. And he would lease from time to time. Sowed 40 acres of wheat and better.

The land was rolling and barren with hardly a tree in sight. In the early days of the Craft homestead, fences were more often used to keep animals out rather than in, because fences were so expensive to build. Fence posts were very precious indeed on this almost treeless prairie, where the only trees were mostly cottonwoods growing along the few streams and intermittent stream courses. Harold (1998) described Horse Creek:

Horse Creek was just west of the [Craft] property [one mile]. It drained an area south of Gate. Hedge apple trees, cottonwoods, and willows lined its bank. There was the Hanging Tree [large cottonwood] also located there on the bank. [I believe] that this [along Horse Creek] is where we got some of our fence posts. Also this is where water came from to fill the tank wagon for the threshing machine [a steam engine].

Grass could be luxuriant and green in the late spring as winter snows melted and spring thunderstorms and warmth gave way to summer heat. Charley Craft, like his neighbors, broke the thick prairie sod with a team of horses and a turning plow, exposing the chestnut brown grassland soils to the surface. The dark, rich color was a product of hundreds of years of prairie grasses that contributed the humus from their roots to the composition of this fertile but thin soil. Fertility was not the problem—it was moisture.

45

The short grass prairie probably should never have been tilled, yet in some years it was incredibly productive for dryland crops, such as wheat, kaffir corn, broomcorn, and sorghum millet. As in all dryland agricultural regions of the world where annual precipitation averages around 20 inches, the Oklahoma Panhandle experiences huge annual variations in precipitation. Sometimes moisture is abundant and sometimes there is a deficit, varying locally by as much as 50 percent or more. When annual precipitation totals fall below 20 inches, most crops become stressed. When the drought lasts for several years, the loose plowed soil may be blown by relentless winds. This part of the Oklahoma Panhandle around Gate and Guymon later was to be the center of the intensive and extensive 1930s' Dust Bowl, locally called The Dirty Thirties.

As daytime summer temperatures rose to 90° F and beyond on the prairie around Gate, so did the rate of evaporation of soil and plant moisture. This climate is known as a middle latitude steppe, with natural vegetation resembling the dry steppe grasslands of the eastern Ukraine. By the end of the summer in this climate, the prairie grasses turn brown, as soil moisture is depleted by increased evaporation.

The natural grass is a prairie bunch grass known as buffalo grass, which forms into a thick grayish-green sod and spreads by forming stolons that creep across the ground. Its blades rise four to six inches high, topped by a burr-like feature that is the female flower. Such species are able to withstand the prolonged droughts of the steppe and heavy grazing even to the ground by foraging animals. Buffalo grass is very hearty because it is has a deep root system. This means that drought stress or over-grazing can destroy virtually all above ground foliage, while the underground core can lie dormant, awaiting the next rain or even the next wet season.

Winter temperatures combined with northerly winds in western Oklahoma created brutal conditions for humans and animals alike. Subzero temperatures and wind speeds greater than 60 mph were common, accounting for the benefits of having the soddy, a bank house partially beneath the ground, or a dugout totally beneath the ground. These houses, made of earth or located beneath the ground, conserved heat in the winter and made the family's living quarters cooler during the height of the summer heat. Because fuel was in such short supply, particularly in the winter, conserving heat was critical.

The steppe grassland, or short-grass prairie, around Gate was just called *prairie* by inhabitants. This prairie was the original home to large native animal species, including bison, deer, antelope, and coyotes. As migratory animals, these creatures were able to survive the droughts, floods, frigid winters, and hot summers by migrating to different locations to lessen the physiological stress on themselves and their environment. By the time homesteaders arrived in the Panhandle, the bison were gone, but there were still occasional sightings of and hunts for deer and antelope. Coyotes remained numerous because, as cropland increased, so did rabbits and rodents.

The most prevalent native animals on the prairies by 1900 were rabbits, skunks and rattlesnakes. Farm families living under rudimentary homestead conditions presented different views of these animals. Rabbits were a welcome fall source of food during homesteaders' first few years. Occasionally, rabbits were even hunted for market. When they became too numerous, however, they ate the homesteaders' crops. Bounties were offered on rabbit ears and occasionally large organized rabbit hunts yielded hundreds of carcasses. W. Guy Parker in *A History of Beaver County* (1971) describes one of the hunts:

> *The Red Cross Committee decided to raise some money with a rabbit drive as there were many rabbits in the county at that time, and a bounty was given for rabbit ears. The contest was held between the east and west part of town, the losers to serve an oyster supper to the winners. There was a two-day drive; the rabbits were sold then to Mr. John Gambs and me for hog feed, each of us taking half. I remember killing 32 rabbits the first day and 35 the second, and one long legged fellow who was with our party of four in the spring wagon killed 45 rabbits the second day. The bounties on these rabbits went to the Red Cross. Men in the (neighboring) Knowles community killed these in 1917. 1100 rabbits weighed 5000 pounds.* (Caption under a picture showing a wagonload of rabbit carcasses and 36 men and boys apparently in the hunting party, *A History of Beaver County*, Vol. II, 1971*) (**Fig. 3.2**).

Skunks were very common and created problems of their own, raiding gardens in the summer and occasionally having altercations with family dogs. Generally, dogs sprayed by skunks were unwelcome around the house for a few days. Skunks also provided meager source of winter income for cash-strapped homesteaders, as skunk hides were in commercial demand in the East. The job of trapping skunks usually fell to young boys who set and tended traps around the family farms.[42]

The open prairie was a particularly difficult place for women, who were often isolated at the house and barn day after day with cooking, making butter, washing, gardening, and taking care of children and animals. Births usually happened in the home, sometimes with a midwife and occasionally with the doctor, assuming he arrived on time. When asked about his mother's experiences on the Oklahoma prairie, Harold (1995) said:

> *I don't think Momma [Martha] ever enjoyed living out there. Really not! I can remember that she never enjoyed it too much . . . it was harsh living. It was rough living.*

What could entice a woman raised with the amenities of a Midwest town to move to a homestead in the Oklahoma Panhandle? Maurie (1995) quoted her grandfather back in Indiana:

> *It was for free [the land] when they filed on the claim . . . her [Martha's] dad told her they [the government] weren't giving much away.*

The Composition of the Craft Family in Gate

The Craft family consisted of Charley, Martha, and ultimately their six children. Two of the six, Paul Vachel (9 July 1896) and Buelah Florina (18 December 1903), were born in Carmel, Indiana, prior to the family's move to Oklahoma. Harriet Maurie (7 July 1907), Cecil Irving (12 May 1909), Harold Newby (12 June 1912), and Forrest Emmanuel (13 November 1914) were born on the farm in Gate, probably attended by Dr. Dougan, the family doctor and close friend. Although the Crafts lived temporarily in

49

Palacios, Texas, from December 1912 through December 1914, no children were born there. Martha, however, became pregnant with Forrest while in Texas.

The bounty collected on these rabbits went to the Red Cross. Men in Knowles community killed these in 1917. 1100 rabbits weighed 5000 pounds.

Fig. 3.2. A rabbit hunt in nearby Knowles Community in 1917. *(Reprinted from A History of Beaver County, Vol. II, Beaver County Historical Society, Inc., 1971, by permission of Dr. Pauline Hodges.)*

The Crafts were close to their Newby relatives. Martha's mother had four sisters, Emma, Lenna, Rachel, and Fleigh (half-sister), and one brother, Lewis. The Crafts were particularly fond of their Aunt Emma Newby Frost, her daughter, Zola (also known as "Frostie"), and son, Arl. Paul Craft was the most prolific writer in the Craft family, and he was a favorite addressee of the Frost family's many postcards to the Crafts, often inquiring about the health and activities of the rest of the family. Paul and, later, his wife, Flossie, preserved more than 100 of these postcards which provide a window into the Craft family's activities in Oklahoma and Texas between 1906 and 1924.[43]

Postcards were very popular in the early 1900s. Members of the Ellis Lineback family in North Carolina occasionally sent cards to Paul, who by this time was a teenager living on the farm in Gate and later in Palacios, Texas. Freda and Eula Lineback wrote cards to Paul, providing a continuing link between Charley and his North Carolina relatives throughout the years in Gate. Sam Craft, Charley's halfbrother, also wrote Paul at least one card—a very friendly card. Sam, at nearly 20 years of age, was more than six years older than Paul in 1909, but he wrote to him as though they were peers.

The Craft Family's Early Years in Gate

Gate, Oklahoma, was a tight community by 1910, not unlike the small Pfafftown, North Carolina, community in which Charley Craft was raised. Gate, a thriving prairie town with a strip of businesses a couple of blocks long, served about 576 families within a two-hour wagon ride in about a six to eight mile circumference **(Fig. 3.3)**. Each quarter section (160 acres) usually contained one family in 1906. The 576 families, averaging five family members each, would have yielded a trade area population of 2,880 people, not including the town's population. The town's trade area was mostly for lower order household and agricultural goods initially, and up until 1920, the town continued to expand. Thereafter, it stagnated and declined. Wayne Lewis (2002) described the population geography of Beaver County across time:

There were 250 children in school in Gate in 1930. Gate had Ford and Chevy dealers, restaurants, [and] two churches—Methodist and Quaker— equally with 100 to 120 people going to Sunday school at each church. Taking the four square miles [four sections] around the Laurence Academy [as an example] in 1905. There was a house on every quarter around the Laurence [Friends] Academy. So there were four houses on every section in 1905. By 1925, half of those were gone. In 1945, half of those [the remainder] were gone. [By] 1965 half of them were gone. By 1985, there was one occupied house in the four square miles. Not unusual. It's not hard to find four square miles in this community [today, 2002], that don't have any houses. By 1990, Gate school had closed and there were 13 kids bused from Gate District and went to school at Laverne. There was one restaurant and an elevator [grain]. If we have more than 25 people in church now, we have a big crowd. Churches stood up better than anything in the country.

Earl and Ada R. Kerns describe the move of the town of Old Gate to the new location:[44]

Gate began around 1902 with a house being built on a site about a mile and a half northwest of the present site of the town. Called Old Gate, between 1903 and 1911, there was a general store with a post office, a State Bank of Commerce, two livery stables, lumber yard, two barber shops, a drugstore, two blacksmith shops, a feed mill, an undertaker establishment combined with a furniture store, real estate office, garage, harness shop, millinery shop, newspaper [Gate Valley Star] and print shop, pool hall, U.S. Land Office, a bakery, and a telephone exchange.

In the spring of 1912 in the aftermath of one of the Panhandle's worst winters on record, the Wichita Falls and Northwestern (WF&N) Railroad arrived in Beaver County from the east. It continued westward to Fogan, Oklahoma, just north of Beaver City, the present county seat. The company, however, bypassed Old Gate, as well as all other existing towns, as was general railroad policy.[45]

Fig. 3.3. Old Gate about 1910. *(Reprinted from A History of Beaver County, Vol. II, Beaver County Historical Society, Inc., 1971, p. 155, by permission of Dr. Pauline Hodges.)*

As Wayne Lewis (2002) and the author traveled from the present site of Gate toward the site of Old Gate, he described the site:

> *Now we are coming to Old Gate. It was a crossroads at the section lines. Here is a cement slab where the printing press was in Old Gate. [The town had] 25 or 30 buildings. They moved all of the buildings from Old Gate to the present Gate. And it was my understanding that they just went straight across [diagonally southwest across the section].*

Rural farm families around Gate produced most of their own food, but they sold cattle and cattle products, hogs, turkeys, chickens, and eggs, as well as wheat and animal feed grains, such as broomcorn and kaffir. Some of the perishable items were sold directly in Gate, such as milk, butter, cheese, and eggs, but the grains were mostly carried by wagon to the railroad at Englewood, Kansas, at least until the railroad came to Gate in 1912.

Commercial establishments in Gate provided items and services not available on the farm, including salt, sugar, coffee, kitchen utensils, and cloth for the household, and hardware and harnesses, implements, and tackle for the farm operation. Purchasing higher-order goods, such as farm equipment and large amounts of lumber and fence posts, for example, required day-long trips to Englewood or Woodward, or a two- to three-day trip to Perryton, Texas.

Most farms around Gate in the early 1900s were largely self-supporting. Spring and early summer gardens produced vegetables that were canned or stored in a root cellar or in the dark recesses of dugouts and bank houses.

Dugouts were simply rooms dug into the ground and covered with a roof, while bank houses were dug into hillsides, exposing one side of the house where a doorway would be located. Water drawn from the well was used in the household and barn and was often reused to irrigate the small garden located near the well. Manure from the barn, spread on the garden during the summer and fall, provided organic fertilizer for pumpkins, potatoes, onions, corn, and beans. All of the family gardens were irrigated with either hand-pumped or windmill-pumped water from hand-dug wells. Isolated farm families yearned for fresh fruits, so many settlers had fruit trees shipped in by railroad to

Englewood, where they were carried by wagon to Gate. Even a few carefully nurtured peach trees sent from Carmel, Indiana, by Martha's father or family provided occasional delicacies for the Craft family, but they had to be irrigated by well water.

Fuel was always a problem, as firewood was virtually unavailable for heating. Consequently, farm families fueled their stoves for heating and cooking either with "buffalo chips," actually dry cow patties, or coal purchased in Englewood. Cattle manure, particularly from the prairie, dried into disks by the sun and wind, making it easy to retrieve, if not covered with snow. This fuel burned very cleanly, with little smoke or soot. It had a high heat output, although it burned quickly. Many farm families considered coal a luxury, but the Crafts apparently used it regularly for cooking. Coal was most certainly a fuel with which Martha had had experience using back in Indiana.[46]

Most heating and cooking by homesteaders in the early days was done on a little topsy stove, which had a small oven attached to the stovepipe. It was an efficient user of fuel, with an adjustable draft on the flue to control the fire and prolong the heat. It could use cow chips, coal, or, on occasion, broomcorn stalks or even straw. A cold winter day might require 20 or more cow chips and a few chunks of coal to minimally heat the house. Conservation of fuel for cooking during lengthy cold periods often meant that the temperatures inside households hovered at only a few degrees above freezing. Few dugouts or bank houses were heated at night, except during the most severe winter weather with high winds. Such conditions sucked heat from even the most protected dugout or bank house.

Collecting buffalo chips was the children's job, requiring daily trips to search around the barn and out onto the prairie every few days to search for new deposits. Generally, the children knew where to search, picking up 10 to 30 chips and stacking them by the door of the house under a small lean-to structure to be used as needed.

After their return to Gate from Palacios, Texas, in 1914, the Crafts bought a Home Comfort Range, which was a much better cook stove than the little topsy stove. This new stove was apparently Martha's pride and joy and made cooking for a family of eight much more manageable than the topsy stove.

The Craft house and barn were situated in the northwest corner of the north half of Section 15, about 100 feet from the western section line road. The lower floor of the structure was dug back into the west bank of a small draw that ran northeast-southwest and connected to the broader east-west valley or draw that crossed the Craft property. The entryway to the lower floor of the dugout faced almost due east. Initially, the lower floor of the bank house was covered with a wooden roof, perhaps sodded, but about 1915, a second aboveground floor was added to accommodate the six Craft children. The size of the lower level was about 10 by 16 feet.

Like most of the Beaver County bank houses constructed at the time, the Craft house initially had a dirt floor, but concrete walls and a floor were soon added, probably a construction technique that Charley learned either in North Carolina or in Indiana. The structure's wall on the east end was wooden, with at least one window and a door opening onto a small raised stoop where dirty shoes could be cleaned and cow chips could be stacked **(Fig.**

3.4). Later, when another floor was added to the house, the front door to that floor was at ground level on the west and faced the road. The east-facing door to the lower story remained the main entryway, but it became the back door to the house after the second story was added. The kitchen and dining area were in the east end of the lower story, while the west end was used as the family's living and sleeping area. When the second story was added, the children slept in two upstairs bedrooms, and Charley and Martha's sleeping quarters remained downstairs **(Fig. 3.5).**[47]

The well was located just uphill and thirty feet to the northeast of the back door of the Craft house. Initially, water from the hand-dug well was hand-drawn, but at some point, a windmill was added, greatly easing the farm work. Charley designed and built a cement trough (or tank) inside the house **(Fig. 3.6)**. The cement was hand-mixed onsite and poured into a wooden frame to harden. The trough was connected to the windmill by a one-inch pipe, where a constant flow of cold ground water provided refrigeration for milk and butter. This was a system similar to a springhouse, with the exception of the windmill, common to farms in North Carolina. Martha kept milk, cheese, butter, and some vegetables stored in crocks sitting in the water-filled trough. Water from the trough drained back eastward to an outside trough and then toward the garden.[48]

The garden was located to the southeast of the back door along the sides of the shallow draw. Thus, the garden had a constant supply of water from a well that Harold (1995) described as "one of the best in the country." Apparently, the family never ran out of water, even during the driest years. Thus, they were able to grow vegetables of all kinds, which Martha and the girls canned for the winter.

Fig. 3.4. Three of the Craft boys sitting on the back steps of the family's bank house on the Craft homestead, circa 1919. Left to right: Forrest (5), Cecil (10), and Harold (7). *(Source: Maurie Craft Lang's family collection, permission by son Martin Lang.)*

Fig. 3.5. The lower story of the Craft bank house, about 10 by 16 feet. A second story frame floor was built on top of the house between 1906 and 1910. *(Photo by author, 2002)*

Outbuildings on the Craft farm included a barn and a chicken and coal storage house. (There is frequent mention of a smokehouse, too, but no evidence of it remains on the site.) The barn, probably first completed during the second year of the homestead in 1906, was located about 125 feet almost due north of the house, also on the east side of the shallow draw. It, too, was a bank structure with the lower story dug back into the bank about 20 feet and about 8 feet wide. Initially, it was likely a single underground story covered with a wooden roof, possibly with sod at least for a few years. By 1910 or 1911, a second wooden story was added, doubling the area under roof. Then the barn's second floor was extended about 12 feet to the west, adding at least a third more area under roof. As with most of the barns with which Charley was familiar, expansion was an ongoing process, where lean-tos and extensions were constantly being added as the money and lumber became available. The extension of the Craft barn westward provided a garage-like feature where machinery could be kept in the dry, as well as a car later on. The barn's loft was used to store grain and fodder for the animals, which were housed in the lower beneath-ground story. This was where the milking was done. A lean-to on the west side of the barn was where the hogs were kept in a pen. The appearance of the Craft barn was amazingly similar in appearance to North Carolina Piedmont barns, particularly the Ellis Lineback barn, with unpainted wood, a lean-to, hay-mow, and equipment storage area (**Fig. 3.7**).

The chicken house/coal storage building was located between the house and barn and was a bank structure, as well, about 8 by 10 feet. Martha kept her chickens and turkeys in this two-story structure (**Fig. 3.8**).[49] Much later a silo was added to the east of the barn.

Fig. 3.6. The author at the Craft homestead site in January 2002. The well and windmill are to the north, the bank house was to the left and the trough, or tank, for chilling food was located to the left of the author and steps. A pipe connecting the windmill and the trough was still visible on this date. *(Photo by Wayne Lewis, 2002)*

Education and Religion Intertwined

Generally, the Craft family's social life in Beaver County revolved around both school and church activities, which were intertwined. The Laurence Friends Academy served the dual purposes, providing both education and religion. School plays and choir performances were at least monthly functions at the schools. The Gate Friends' (Quakers') religious services were held in the Academy building where classes were provided to enrolled students. Wayne Lewis (2002) describes the Quakers:

Since the Quakers had no paid minister, they could have "meetings" with little overhead and organization. Other church-oriented neighbors joined with them.

Fig. 3.7. Two of three farmstead outbuildings on the Craft farm, circa 1920. Note the 1917 Ford touring car inside the barn. On the reverse of this picture, Martha had written about the chicken house to the right: "Chicken house (where) hen turkeys roosted. Coal was at east end of chicken house. When one boy would fight off the gobler (sic) while the others put coal in the buckets." *(Source: Maurie Craft Lang's family collection, permission by son Martin Lang.)*

Martha was the family member with the closest connection to the Quaker Church. She was raised a Quaker in Indiana. Through this connection to the Quakers, she and Charley were linked to Henry Fellow and his efforts to bring Quakers to settlements in Kansas, Oklahoma, and southeast Colorado. When the Crafts, Cards, and Smiths arrived in Gate in the spring of 1905, the first order of business was to help establish their religion.[50]

Fig. 3.8. Martha Craft feeding her turkeys, which she raised as "egg money" to provide extras for the children, circa 1922. Note the unpainted North Carolina Piedmont-style barn with a lean-to to the left and a silo and chicken house to the right. *(Source: Maurie Craft Lang's family collection, permission by son Martin Lang.)*

Martha, rather than Charley, along with the other Quakers in the Gate settlement, helped push for a Quaker academy (high school) immediately upon the family's arrival in Gate. Exactly what role Martha and the others played in following through with the effort to build

Laurence Friends Academy is not clear, even from Henry Fellow's memoirs. It appears that it was Henry Fellow's idea and initiation, but the Quaker community made it happen **(Figs. 3.9 and 3.10)**. Cory L. Morgan in *A History of Beaver County (1971)* says:

> *This early Beaver County group solved this latter problem [house of worship] in 1905 by erecting a building for use as a meetinghouse and also as an academy. This [Laurence Friends Academy] was for several years the only State accredited High School west of Woodward in Oklahoma.*

Henry Fellow approached ranchers and farmers in Beaver County to solicit funds to build the academy. Education was a major issue for not only the Quakers, but for other large and growing families around the territory. There were no accredited high schools in the territory at that time, but ranchers and settlers realized that schools were critical for their children's education.

A homesteader, Laurence Tom Kersey, donated the land for the meetinghouse and first academy building.[51]

Most people around Gate knew that Martha was a strong promoter of the Academy. Charley was a supporter too, but he was not as religious as was Martha. Jeanne Carpenter Baker (1995) said:

> *. . . Grandpa Craft [Charley] was not Quaker. It was Grandma Craft [Martha] that was a Quaker. Grandpa Craft came from the Moravians [of North Carolina]).*[52]

Actually, Charley was raised as a Methodist in the Rev. Daniel and Theresa Doub household. The Reverend was a Methodist pastor in the Doub Chapel Methodist Church located just north of Pfafftown, North Carolina. Charley's father, Junius, and stepmother, Martha Styers Craft, were also lifetime Methodists, as were most of his North Carolina relatives by 1900.

Fig. 3.9. Supporters of Laurence Friends Academy, Gate, Oklahoma, circa 1906. It appears that Martha Craft may be in the front row, fifth from the right in dark dress. *(Source: Maurie Craft Lang's family collection, permission by son Martin Lang.)*

Fig. 3.10. The faculty, supporters, and student body of Laurence Friends Academy, Gate, Oklahoma, circa 1906. *(Source: Maurie Craft Lang's family collection, permission by son Martin Lang.)*

The Moravians out of Pennsylvania settled nearby Salem (Winston-Salem), Bethania, and Bethabra, and the Moravian Church was strong within Forsyth County. In fact, some of the Moravian settlers joined the Moravian Church in the 1700s because there was free Moravian land available in North Carolina, settling on some of this land around Bethania and Salem. By 1900, few of the North Carolina Craft descendents still claimed to be Moravians, most having become Methodists.

Although raised a Methodist, Charley apparently took the Quaker faith upon marrying Martha. Maurie (1995) was certain that Henry Fellow was the strength behind the Quaker settlement in Beaver County and said:

> *But Henry Fellow was the contact with Grandma Craft. He came out and started the Academy. He headquartered out of the University—there out of the Friends University in Wichita, Kansas. He knew the red tape that you had to go through to get it [started].*

Harold (1995) agreed, but pointed out that, if not for the Cards, Smiths, and Crafts, the Academy might not have been built:

> *I think he [Henry Fellow] was a wonderful man. But he wasn't the determining factor in opening . . . the Laurence Friends Academy. . . . Grandma Craft—yes, she was one of them. John Card, Max and May Smith, Charles and Martha Craft. Well, nobody got credit for building it [because it was a community effort].*

Building the Laurence Friends Academy was especially important to Martha. Not only did it formalize a place for the community to worship and to socialize, but also she and Charley wanted to have a nearby school to educate their growing family. Paul, who was already nine years old in 1905, would be the first Craft child to attend the Academy four years later. Education was very important in Quaker tradition, and Martha, no doubt with Charley's support, was a vocal supporter of building the Academy. Through the years, four of Martha and Charley's six children attended the Academy: Paul, Buelah, Cecil, and Maurie. Harold and Forest were not old enough to attend high school before the Crafts left Gate in 1924.

Building the Laurence Friends Academy was a huge effort undertaken by the Quaker community, which at no time was more than one-third to one-half of the area's population. Yet, the school was open to students of all denominations. Quoting Cory L. Morgan again:

> This tuition and donation financed school venture, though under the management and direction of the Friends [Quaker] church, was nonetheless wholly undenominational in its educational offering, as it followed strictly the State curricular requirements. . . . Probably no event in the history of early Beaver County had more impact and favorable influence on its citizens than this Laurence Friends Academy and the scholarship of the graduating students body . . . and in those early days the letters L.F.A. was an insignia of educational superiority on any student's record, and the diploma from the school was held in as high esteem in that era as a college degree is of now.

The Laurence Friends Academy was located on the northwest corner of Sec. 15, T5, R28. The Academy discontinued operation in 1924, the very year that the Crafts departed Gate. The area's population decline, its aging population, and the construction of a public high school all contributed to its closing. After the Craft family departed for the Denver area, Maurie stayed behind in Gate to finish the final academic year of her high school education at the Academy. She roomed with a nearby family, but had what she described as a "bad experience" in her living arrangements during these last few months. We know little about this experience, except that Maurie felt uncomfortable in the company of a male in the household where she was staying.[53]

Cecil and Forrest also stayed behind in Gate. Cecil was 16 and attended the Academy for all but the last month or so of his first year in high school. Forrest was only nine years old and in the third grade. After the sale of the farm, Martha took the two boys by train to join Charley, Harold, Buelah, and Jeanne in Denver.

When this author visited the Laurence Friends Academy site in 2002 in the accompaniment of Wayne Lewis, there was absolutely no evidence that two large buildings, an administration building and girls' dormitory, had occupied the site nearly 100 years earlier.[54]

The Craft family faithfully attended the Friends' worship service, remembered Wayne Lewis:

> *He [Charley Craft] was honest and he was a church person. He helped with the Academy [to] keep it going.*

67

Throughout their elementary school years, the Craft children attended Gate School or Union Center School, District # 4. Before Gate was relocated in 1913, Old Gate was two and a half miles south of the Craft house. After the town moved, New Gate was almost four miles southwest. Union Center School, often called the Maphet School because homesteader Charlie Maphet donated the land, was located only about a mile northeast of the Craft farm. Based on distance to school, the younger Craft children more than likely attended Union Center School. At least by 1921, however, Harold (nine years old) and Forrest (six years old) attended a little school called the Berends School, located three miles northwest of the homestead. It was closer than the New Gate School, but was still farther away than Union Center. Perhaps the reason Charley and Martha sent them to the Berends School rather than the Union Center School or Gate may have been that they could accompany their older sister, Buelah. As it turned out, Buelah taught there for a short while and was Harold and Forrest's teacher for at least a half year. It is unclear where Cecil attended elementary school, but he did not go to the Berends School with Harold and Forrest during 1921-22.[55]

CHAPTER 4

SEASONAL RHYTHMS ON THE PRAIRIE

Beaver County's Weather, 1904-1924

Not only is Beaver County's weather erratic, but so too is its climate. Weather consists of short-term atmospheric conditions, as with daily, weekly, or monthly temperatures and precipitation. Climate, on the other hand, is long-term averages or totals of weather conditions over lengthier periods of time, as in seasons, years, decades, or centuries.

Farmers rely upon a combination of weather conditions conducive to producing successful crops. Successful cropping seasons in the Oklahoma Panhandle particularly depend upon sufficient rainfall spread throughout the growing season. Of course, in addition to weather conditions, other critical variables such as heat and cold, wind, and extreme weather events also determine the success or failure of a crop.

The successes of the Craft farm and the family's finances depended upon the weather before and during the growing season. Good crop years meant that the family could buy a few extras; poor crop years meant that they had to "make do" with what they had.

In dryland regions of the world, like the Oklahoma Panhandle, precipitation can be very erratic. In fact, the drier the climate, the more erratic is the precipitation. Without irrigation, for example, wheat requires 20 inches of precipitation and the precipitation should optimally be spread through the period from November through June. If the majority of the annual precipitation for wheat came after harvest or in the early fall, it only marginally helped the following year's crop, if at all. The world's steppe climates, which are semi-arid, are notoriously fickle in their precipitation and, consequently, in their wheat harvests. Precipitation, especially in the late spring and early summer, can consist of scattered thundershowers, wetting one farm but not the neighboring farm. Brief, heavy downpours from thunderstorms, as opposed to gentle soaking regional rains, often result in heavy runoff. Although weather conditions may average out over the years, there may still be considerable differences in precipitation benefits from farm to farm in any given year.

Snowfall is an issue in providing moisture for crops—particularly wheat—in the Oklahoma Panhandle. In general, 10 to 12 inches of snow are equivalent to one inch of water. The advantage of snow is that it tends to melt slowly and contributes considerably to soil moisture. However, on the open prairie, wind tends to drift snow, leaving bare soil in exposed places and greater snow accumulations in protected places. Furthermore, under sudden warm and windy conditions, snow may sublimate, or evaporate, without going through the liquid stage, thus contributing little to soil moisture. Nonetheless, winters with heavy snowfalls tend to produce good wheat crops in middle latitude dry-land regions. Snowfall can vary a great deal on the Oklahoma prairie, with some years having hardly any at all. Such is the erratic behavior of precipitation in semi-arid locations. It was a gamble every year for the Oklahoma homesteaders.

Winter wheat is planted in the fall of the year throughout the southern Great Plains, typically sprouting during the late fall, lying fairly dormant through the winter, and heading up in late spring and early summer. Although some moisture is necessary and desirable in the fall for the plants to sprout, the critical period for moisture occurs during the months of February through May, when wheat plants are growing. December, January, and February snows are important, as well, because they help store moisture, releasing it into the soil days or weeks after falling.

No reliable crop production data exists for Beaver County in the first two decades of 1900, when the Crafts were farming there. No records at all were kept on crop production on the Craft farm during the period. Meteorological data, however, can be used to make some general assessments of moisture availability to crops and the potential for crop success during the years the Crafts lived in Oklahoma.

The Oklahoma Climatological Survey provided this author with monthly weather data for Beaver County, Oklahoma, for the period between 1904 and 1924.[56] The author analyzed the data using a simple triage method to determine the best precipitation conditions for winter wheat. Monthly precipitation totals above and below the monthly means from January through May, the critical growing season for winter wheat, regardless of annual totals, were calculated (**Table 1**). Years with at least one month of exceptional moisture and/or three months at or near the monthly means were classified as "good years." Years with no more than one month's precipitation total above the monthly mean, but not excessively above the mean, were assumed to be "poor years." The remaining years, with only two months slightly above the mean, were considered "moderate years." Data for 1905 and 1906 were incomplete, although the data for the first four months of 1905 were available. Snowfall totals were included in the data as water equivalent inches.

Based upon precipitation alone for the 18 years between 1907 and 1924, there were six "wet (or good) years," six "normal (or moderate) years," and six "dry (or poor) years" in Beaver County. With the omitted data for 1906, the wet years were 1911, 1912, 1915, 1922, 1923, and 1924. Normal years were 1907, 1909, 1917, 1918, 1919, and 1921. The dry years were 1908, 1910, 1913, 1914, 1916, and 1920. Normal years were not failures at all, as they met the normal expectations of the farmers. Dry years, particularly when they occurred back-to-back, as in 1913 and 1914, were devastating to the homesteaders.

The rhythms of wet and dry years appear to have influenced several of the Crafts' decisions. For example, 1912 seems to have been an incredible crop year, following the blizzards that dumped 42.2 inches of snow between January and April. The abundant crop that likely resulted that summer on the Craft farm may have helped convince a buyer to purchase it. The following year, 1913, however, was likely a crop disaster with only one month having slightly more than normal precipitation. The buyer of the Craft farm defaulted on his note, probably as a result of this dry year.

Cold, Brutal Winters

Winters on the prairie for homesteaders were brutal. The wind might blow from nearly any direction in the Oklahoma Panhandle, as cold and warm fronts passed. The passage of intense cold fronts brought northerly high winds accompanied by extremely low temperatures to the open prairie.

TABLE 1

Precipitation Variations from the Monthly Norm, 1904-1924, Beaver County, Oklahoma (inches). *Source: Monthly data provided by Howard Johnson, Oklahoma Climatological Survey, University of Oklahoma.*

Year	Jan	Feb	Mar	Apr	Mar	June	July	Aug	Sept	Oct	Nov	Dec	Total
1904	-0.46	-0.29	-0.69	-1.26	-0.83	3.73	2.22	-0.44	-0.67	-0.62	-0.27	0.01	-0.57
1905	0.12	-0.17	1	2.45					1.49	0.1			
1906						1.49	1.11	1.87	2.86	2.56			
1907	1.1	-0.27	-0.69	-1.55	-0.78	2.3	-0.22	-0.46					
*1908		0.72	-0.69	-0.65	-2.29	1.55	-3.12	-0.94	-0.08	-0.88	-0.64	-0.69	
1909	-0.49	0.27	1.51	-1.96	-0.69	1.16	-1.24	-0.73	-0.76	-0.74	5.64	-0.29	2.63
*1910	0.13	0.46	-0.64	0.21	-1.87	1.76	0.15	4.2	-2.04	-0.97	-0.56	-0.16	-2.82
1911	-0.45	4.23	-0.25	-1.39	-0.41	-2.72	-0.41	0.9	-1.14	-0.1	-0.56	3.52	1.49
1912	-0.04	2.23	0.62	-0.5	-2.01	1.86	-0.95	0.2	0.8	-0.93	-0.99	-0.58	-0.3
*1913	-0.2	0.78	-0.51	-0.75	-0.88	-0.87	-0.51	-0.72	1.81	-0.78	0.85	0.85	-0.82
*1914	-0.6	-0.25	-0.33	-0.9	1.52	-2.23	0.81	2.15	-1.65	0.53	-1.19	-0.25	-2.39
1915	-0.08	1.96	-0.17	2	2.06	-0.16	-0.32	0.27	5.73	1.3	-1.12	-0.43	10.14
*1916	-0.25	-0.32	-0.6	-0.02	-1.21	3.85	-2.67	-1.17	-0.9	-1.12	-1.19	0.22	-4.57
*1917	-0.5	0.19	-0.62	-0.04	1.27	-0.86	-1.94	3.28	-0.13	-1.17	-0.42	-0.53	-4.01
1918	-0.1	-0.28	0.45	-1.27	1.48	-0.4	-1.11	-1.45	2.79	0.47	-0.68	3.32	3.22
*1919	-0.6	0.84	0.39	-0.87	-0.61	-1.82	-0.11	2.03	-1.39	-0.52	-0.29	-0.57	-3.52
*1920	-0.27	-0.36	-0.45	-1.03	0.09	-1.88	0.51	-0.67	0.05	5	-0.19	0.35	1.69
1921	0.25	1.09	-0.7	-1.37	-1.23	-0.24	1.04	1.15	-0.3	-1.15	-1.19	-0.03	5
1922	-0.05	1.13	3.8	-0.8	1.55	0.15	-0.05	-0.57	-0.85	-1.04	-0.88	-0.56	-1.27
1923	-0.6	-0.04	-0.18	0.36	3.29	2.23	-2.08	-1.81	1.96	9.08	0.04	0.49	12.74
1924	-0.37	-0.52	2.66	-0.37	-1.74	-1.79	-0.62	-0.73	-1.25	0.73	-0.54	0.04	-4.5

*Indicates dry years.

Exceptional wind chills caused by high wind and low temperatures could be deadly to both humans and their animals. Harold (1996) remembered how bad the weather could be:

> *Well, I've known the time, seen the snow so bad out there. My dad having to get to town to get groceries and [took] the bed off the wagon, the flat box, grain bed off the wagon. He and the neighbor put [the bed] on planks and [made] a sled. And hitched up a team of draft horses and used it to go to town on the sled. This would have been in the early, early '20s or during the war, or thereabouts World War I.*

The worst winter that the Craft family endured in Gate was undoubtedly the one in the winter of 1911-12, just prior to their selling the farm in Oklahoma and moving to Texas. Beginning in December 1911 and lasting until April 1912, blizzard after blizzard battered the region, leaving cattle frozen and roads closed to wagons for weeks at a time. People ran out of home heating fuel and they had to walk to Englewood to buy coal at the railhead there.

Dots and Dashes, the official publication of the Morse Telegraph Club, Inc. reported[57]

> *Early settlers remember the winter of 1911-12 as one of the worst experiences. [In] a storm a week before [Christmas], a three-day blizzard dumped 24 inches of snow on the area and before the huge wind-driven drifts had a chance to thaw, succeeding storms in January and again later in February added to the snow cover. It was late March before*

the last drift was gone. All that winter, men and mules fought snow and cold to prepare a roadbed for a long-awaited rail line into the Panhandle area. Work had begun late summer 1911 to drive the Wichita Falls and Northwestern northward out of Hammond on the border of Roger Mills and Custer Counties to the southeast of Harper County. The camp foreman was Mr. Whisenant. His wife cooked for the crew, which was comprised of about 20 men. Supplies were wagon freighted from Englewood, Kansas. During the worst of the winter weather, the workers were marooned in their tents for three weeks one time, unable to do anything but care for their stock. Meanwhile, the men near Laverne were having worst problems. Their tents were blown down during the storm of February 20. Luckily, a farmer lived nearby. The man helped drive the crew's livestock into his barns and sledded them [took the workers by sled] to his own home for shelter.[58]

Most families around Gate did not have enough coal to last through such a long and difficult winter. Heavy and drifting snow covered most of the cow chips and even those that could be found were frozen rather than dried. People became desperate for fuel. Wayne Lewis (2002) remembered:

Folks who lived on the road between Gate and Englewood [Kansas] said that during that stormy weather [1911-12], you could see somebody on the road any time you were looking. They were going to Englewood and coming back with coal. They would get the road broken out and the wind would fill it full [snow drifts] the next night. So they had to break the roads every day. In those days, their houses weren't insulated.

There are many interesting stories about this and other dangerous blizzards in the Oklahoma Panhandle during the late 1800s and early 1900s. It was not unusual for people to be caught unexpectedly in a blizzard and had to find shelter wherever they could. Local people, however, had a history of sharing their shelters and food with the unfortunate during these storms. Harold related a story in 1995 that he had heard from his father, Charley:

This John Card was a tall guy. Real tall guy. I don't know whether my dad was with him at the time or not. But it kinda seems like the story goes that the two of them were together when going across there [the prairie]. It was real cold. They had stopped along the way to get inside when a storm hit them. And they saw smoke arising out of the ground. They went by where they [saw] this smoke was in order to get inside. And sure enough there was a fellow a living in this dugout. So they told the man their predicament. And the man said, "Why, yes." He didn't have much, but for them to come in and get inside and spend the night. So when they went to bed down in there, why it was cold inside even. It was one of these storms like they get out there in western Oklahoma at times. So he put John Card to sleep in one of the beds he had. What it was, was a dugout in one of the walls that was just hollowed out in the wall, which was back in a bank [further back]. It had just [been] hollowed out back in there far enough for a shelf for a guy to get into. It [the dugout] was lined with

*logs kind of on the inside. It [the bed] was too
small for John card to lay in, so he had to sit up
all night. But it [the dugout] was lined with logs
anyway. They had a small kind of a potbelly stove
to keep warm . . . . Well, my dad was a shorter
guy than John Card. Him [Card] being so tall
he couldn't sleep [in that short bed]. So he got
up. The next morning when my dad and this man
got up out of one of these [places] . . . John Card
had taken a hatchet and peeled all the logs on the
inside and used the bark to burn. Peeled the logs
on the inside on this guy's log cabin to burn to
keep warm all night long.*

Refreshing But Frightening Springs

Most of the precipitation falling around Gate,
Oklahoma, was from snow in the wintertime and rainfall,
hail, or late snow during the springtime. As winter snows
melted and spring moisture added, soil moisture was stored
for the spring and summer growing season. If winters and
springs passed without leaving at least 10 inches or so of
moisture equivalent, crops particularly suffered.

Spring on the Great Plains is notorious for severe
weather. Generally associated with frontal systems
radiating from low-pressure systems passing from west to
east across the United States, strong spring storms bring
wind, rain and frequently damaging hail. Harold (1995)
remembered a boyhood experience with a hailstorm:

*I remember being in one of those [school]
programs one night . . . when one of those hail
storms we're talking about hit. And, of course, we*

had gaslights. We were there and this program was just starting. Most of the people were traveling by horse and buggy. But, anyway, I remember the program being broken up by a wicked hailstorm. And the first thing you know [bangs on the table with his fist], *a hunk of ice come through the window about the size of a brick and hit a table like that and glanced across the room and hit one of the desks. The lights went out and everybody was in there in the dark. The clouds began hailing. I am telling you that was the worst hailstorm! The lightning—it just shaked that whole building. And when the hail storm was over, they had kind of a place where you parked your horses [and they] could stand under a shed out there. [We loaded on] our flatbed wagon and started home . . . at the end of the field, you could look down and all that just looked like a lake across there because those [furrows] between the [plowed, or listed] ridges [in the field] were all full of water and ice*[59].

The most frightening spring phenomenon for homesteaders, however, was the tornado. Toward the end of winter in early March, days begin to warm on the Oklahoma Panhandle and the propensity for tornadoes moves from the Gulf Coast increasingly northward into the Great Plains. These storms are normally associated with the passage of cold fronts and the squall lines that precede cold fronts during the spring. Tornadoes typically track from southwest to northeast across the region and, with their intensely concentrated winds, can do great damage in their paths, particularly to above-ground structures. Many barns, for example, parts of which were aboveground structures in Beaver County in the early 1900s, often had wind damage from tornadoes and intense microbursts.

Strong winds in early spring on the Oklahoma prairie are often from the south. These winds circulate counterclockwise around low-pressure cells moving eastward across the Great Plains. Although these are not necessarily dust storms, these strong winds often carry abundant dust particles. In combination, the wind and dust create a surprising local vegetative response by deforming the few cottonwood trees on the landscape into a form called *krumholz*. Trees that are *krumholzed* have their crests pointing downwind—in this case, northward. The blasting of the dust particles against the spring buds on the cottonwoods "trains" them to grow away from the wind. Similar forms are seen around the world wherever dominant winds from one direction, combined with sand, dust, or ice crystals, literally train trees' new growth to point away from the source of the wind.

On Oklahoma's prairie, *krumholzed* cottonwoods create a landscape signature that says much about the conditions under which homesteaders had to live day in and day out **(Fig. 4.1)**.

Long Hot Summers

Typical summers on the Oklahoma prairie are hot and dry. Relative humidity tends to be very low, creating drying conditions for both natural vegetation and crops. As soil moisture declines, plants quickly become stressed by hot, dry, and persistent winds.

Local scattered summer thunderstorms may bring precipitation as intense but short-lived rainfall events. Occasionally, however, these storms become large meso-storms that can drop several inches of rain in a very brief time, often accompanied by hail. Such storms create intense runoff, even on moderate slopes, as the rate of precipitation may be several times greater than the soil's ability to absorb it. This is typical of the precipitation regime in dryland regions of the world, where conditions are either "boom or bust" for farmers. Even during dry years, these intense "cloudbursts" may bring copious amounts of precipitation of short durations so that the rapid precipitation may do little or nothing to break a drought.

Fig. 4.1. Most cottonwoods in Beaver County have the krumholtz characteristic, whereby spring wind accompanied by dust and sometimes ice "train" new growth to be away from the wind. In Beaver County, most trees "point" toward the north. *(Photo by Wayne Lewis, 2003.)*

Farmers universally fear hailstorms. Hailstorms may occur in the spring, associated with the passage of fronts and squall lines, or in the summer, associated with afternoon and evening thunderstorms and with large meso-storms. Summer hailstorms are particularly disastrous for farmers' crops as plants near maturity. Although hail does little harm to wheat at the early stages of growth in the spring, when a hailstorm comes during wheat's mature stage in the summer, it can destroy an entire year's crop. In fact, because of the scattered nature of summer thunderstorms, hail may decimate one farmer's wheat crop while leaving the neighbor's crop undamaged. The Craft family experienced flood, wind, and hail damage frequently.[60]

Dust storms were prevalent in the late spring and summer. The worst dust storms of the century in the Oklahoma Panhandle, of course, occurred during the Dust Bowl of the 1930s, but there were occasional dust storms about every second or third year earlier in the century. Preceded by rolling, dark clouds from the west or southwest, the dust-laden wind would arrive quite suddenly, typically lasting only a matter of hours, or perhaps a day. The sun would be partially blotted out, and fine dust would enter everything. Homesteaders had to shake the dust out of bed linens, but a "gritty feeling" remained on the sheets. Caught on the open prairie, people would be forced to cover their mouths and noses with handkerchiefs. Cattle would turn their tails to the wind and seek shelter in draws or behind structures, if available.

Harold (1995) had experienced first-hand his mother's reaction to dust storms on the prairie:

I remember, in our house [at Gate] and she [my mother] was a good housekeeper . . . shaking the sheets out before we would go to bed at night and shaking the sand out. . . . The sheets would be just full of sand [and] the air would be full of dust. It got worse after we got out [of Oklahoma in 1924].

Perhaps the greatest danger from blowing dust was long-term exposure, which could exacerbate lung problems, particularly for asthmatics and tuberculosis patients. Tuberculosis was quite common all across the country in the early 1900s. Some patients came to the Panhandle to seek a cure in the dry air, but most found the dust and cold winters exacerbated their pulmonary problems.[61]

Meat for the Winter

Around October each year following the first hard freeze, the Crafts would slaughter at least one or two hogs for pork and a cow for beef. "Hog killings," as they were universally called across the country in the early 1900s, were festive occasions when several hogs would be killed, dressed, and preserved.

Harold (1995) loved to talk about the family's winter preparations and particularly how his dad and mother prepared meat for the family:

Besides what they [the family] butchered and smoked down, they packed in barrels lots of hogs. My dad would be butchering for the wintertime. They would put away for winter. They would butcher lots of hogs and put it in these big oak barrels. Well, maybe salt-cured. He had a big smokehouse. We smoked a lot of meat. We raised our own beef [and ate] our own beef all of the time. There was lots of meat all the time.

A couple of neighbors would typically arrive to help, as water was boiled in large black pots, fired by cow chips, corn stalks and straw, and coal. A large white-and-black Poland China hog would be led near the barn, shot in the head, its throat cut and the blood saved for blood pudding. Using a block and tackle attached to a gimble stick between its hind legs, the hog would be dipped in a vat of hot water for a few seconds, and the hair would be scrapped off with knives and metal scrapers.

The hog would be "dressed," meaning the removal of the internal organs. Slitting the hog's brisket from throat to anus, the butcher would guide the organs into a washtub. The tub would typically be carried to a table where the women would work to sort out the various organs for use. The heart and liver were delicacies to be cooked and consumed within a few days. The intestines were cleaned and washed by hand as casings for sausage stuffing. Fat was rendered to lard by boiling down the pieces, leaving cracklings treasured by the children and adults alike. Lard was often stored in lard cans, but some would be used in the canning process to preserve certain cuts of pork. Hams were typically rubbed with salt and pepper, wrapped in brown paper and cotton cloth, and hung in a cool place to cure. Even the hog's brains were a delicacy when cooked as brains and eggs for breakfast. Hog jowl and pickled pig's feet were also table fare. Some pork was smoked, as was the tradition in North Carolina, but the source or type of wood used is not known.

A yearling cow was handled much the same way. However, the cow would be skinned rather than scraped, making it a far simpler operation. Preserving beef was much more problematic than pork. Much of the beef had to be canned, as salt does not cure beef as well as it does pork. Nonetheless, keeping the beef hanging in temperatures below 45 or 50 degrees Fahrenheit allowed it to age naturally. Beef, unlike pork, could not be kept into the warm temperatures of late spring or summer without spoilage.

Although Martha occasionally cooked one of her prized turkeys, generally they were considered commercial livestock on the farm. Turkeys were valuable, and they, unlike other domestic fowl, could be driven on foot to market in a pinch.

Harold (1995) enjoyed talking about how the family made its money and how Charley and Martha worked together to make the family's living:

> *My mom had a bunch of chickens all of the time. [She] had lots of eggs and sold eggs and chickens. I remember they had turkeys. Had a big turkey crop every fall. Grew cattle. Sold lots of cattle every fall. Probably milked 10 to 15 head all of the time. Sold cream. Separated cream and sold cream. Made butter only for our own use, but sold the cream in five and ten gallon cans. And had the big cream separator. We lived three and a quarter miles from town. Now, I don't know whether they [Charley and Martha] took it every Saturday or whether they went on schedule down to Gate or*

what. But then I know they sold lots of cream. Lots of it. Fed milk to hogs. They had a big hog crop every year.

Chickens were considered a crucial source of protein "on the hoof," so to speak, for farm families. At any given time, Martha had 25 to 50 chickens—mostly laying hens, but including one rooster and several young chickens for boiling or frying. In addition, there would be a dozen small chicks accompanying several "mother hens." Chickens were generally allowed to roam the barnyard during the day foraging for grain and insects, often picking undigested grain from the cattle manure and catching insects in the garden nearby. A few handfuls of cracked wheat, oats, or corn and a few table scraps made up the daily diet of the flock, supplemented with an occasional handful of crushed limestone to assure that the eggshells would be hard.

Chickens roosted at night inside the barn on partitions between the cattle stalls or in their chicken coops. Hens laid their eggs in nests in the hay in the barn or inside their coops. Coops were rough enclosures made of wood about 2- by 4- feet, setting off the ground by the barn and, apparently, at one time directly east of the bank house, where overflow water from the cooling trough inside the house could be used to water the poultry. This location also made the protection of the chickens and the gathering of eggs easier for the family. Local predators included coyotes and skunks during the night and hawks during the day. Inside the coops would be perches for the chickens and boxes for the nests.

Fresh eggs also were critical to farm families' protein intake. It was a daily chore for the children of the family to search for and gather eggs for the family. Most of the younger children found this to be a pleasant and entertaining chore, not unlike an Easter egg hunt, especially when the chickens would nest in the barn. A couple of the hens at any time would be "setting hens," staying on their nests almost continuously to hatch new chicks, replacing those being used as dinner fare.

Chickens also were small units that could be killed, dressed, and cooked in slightly over an hour. Because they were small units, chickens provided meat for "company," the occasional visitor, or for picnics at church events. They could be fried or stewed. As stewed chicken, the dish could be served as a soup, dumplings, or pie. Chickens, canned beef, and cured pork made up the majority of the family's summer protein, while occasional fresh beef and pork would be available during the late fall and winter.

Killing a chicken simply meant reaching into the coop through a partially opened door, grabbing the chicken of choice by the leg, and dragging it out while closing the gate behind. There were two ways to dispatch the chicken: wringing its neck or chopping its head off with an ax. The choice depended upon the person in charge, as some were more squeamish with one tactic over the other. Wringing meant grabbing the chicken by the neck and swinging its body in a tight circle until the neck was broken, generally about five quick circles. Care had to be taken not to swing too hard, or the chicken's head might be severed from the body. Too little swinging, on the other hand, would not break the chicken's neck.

Cutting off the chicken's head required a special technique to quiet the bird. Usually, the chicken's head would be pushed under one wing, then, holding the chicken's body between two hands out in front of his body, the dispatcher would move the bird around and around in about ten tight circles, dizzying the bird. Then grasping the chicken by the legs, he would lay the chicken's head on a chopping block, sever it with a single blow from an ax, and immediately toss the chicken's body into the barnyard. The headless chicken would flop about for about a minute.

"Dressing a chicken" meant removing its feathers and preparing it for cooking. Generally, dipping the headless chicken for a moment into hot water loosened the feathers, and then the feathers could be picked off. Finally, the chicken was held over an open fire for a few moments to singe the tiny "pin" feathers. The chicken would be gutted, a process that usually took place in the barnyard. But there were two internal delicacies—the liver and gizzard—which had to be saved, cleaned, and fried.

The chicken was of compact size as a source of meat, and it played a critical role on the farm. More often than not, chickens were sold only locally, as every farm had some chickens. There was not a distant market for chickens as there was for turkeys. Chickens provided a quick meal, ready for the table easily within an hour or two.

Commercial Livestock

Cattle were the main commercial livestock raised on the Craft farm, but selling chickens and turkeys and their eggs was an important source of income for Martha. Considered "egg money," this income was used to purchase clothes and shoes and a few luxury items for the house. In poor crop years, this income became doubly important to the household. According to Harold (1995):

*. . . they [the Craft family] had plenty of milk,
plenty of chickens, plenty of cream, plenty of eggs.
I think [they began to raise] turkeys immediately.
. . . They raised hundreds of them . . . put them in a
big double deck wagon box. . . . [They] took them
by horse and wagon to Englewood, Kansas, and
sold them at the railhead. It was during World War
I, sure. . . . And the folks raised lots of turkeys.
A hundred turkeys was nothing. And we raised
all our own feed. I remember lots of time, many
a day, grinding. We had our own grinder that was
operated by horses. You hitched the horses up [to]
a circular grinder. And poured grain in the top of
it and scooped it out of the bottom.*

The Cimarron Territory was cattle country prior to
the squatters coming in the late 1800s and the homesteaders
in the early 1900s. When the land was homesteaded, cattle
continued to make up a large part of the farming effort
for the homesteaders, but the way they were raised had
changed. When the Territory was open range, there were
no fences and cattle were branded, so they could range
for many miles across the prairie seeking shelter, water,
and the best forage of buffalo grass. Cattle were grazed
on the open range to take advantage of "free" grazing
and to produce animals that could be driven in herds to
a railhead and sent to slaughterhouses. The end product
was beef, though stringy and tough compared to today's
beef because of the cow's diet, its forced march, and its
breed. Hearty Texas longhorn cattle, originally brought to
Mexico from Spain, were the choice of ranchers through
the late 1800s. As the land was settled, however, open
range grazing declined and cattle drives became fewer
and fewer.

When homesteaders occupied and eventually fenced their land, their cattle could no longer range away from the farm to seek grazing. Farmers had to change strategies in order to produce cattle for commercial purposes. In fact, cattle began to serve two commercial purposes: providing meat and milk products. By about 1910, the only cattle drives were by buyers who bought cattle from the homesteaders and made short drives to the railhead at Englewood, which would have been by the Craft house in Gate, traveling north toward one of the stream fords on the Cimarron River.[62]

The Cimarron River occasionally presented a major barrier to cattle drives into the 1920s. The river's flashiness meant that travelers sometimes wouldn't know from one day to the next whether the river would be swollen when they arrived there with their herds. That wasn't the only problem associated with crossing the Cimarron with a herd of cattle.

Harold (1995) remembered episodes involving the cattle drives, particularly during dry periods, when farmers had to sell off some of their cattle:

I do remember cattle drives coming by. It had started getting so dry [and] it had been so long since they [cattle] had had anything to drink. When they hit the first water hole on the Cimarron River . . . the first cattle piled in to the edge of the river and the cattle behind them piled in on top of them. As I remember, it looked to me like there was 20 or 30 cattle had drowned because the cattle had followed behind them [circa 1918].

When settlement of the open range began, range cattle often overran farmers' crops. Initially, fences erected by homesteaders kept animals out of their crops rather than fencing the cattle in. Buelah (1988) remembered hearing or reading about conflicts between the homesteaders and cattlemen:

> When this creek [Horse] was settled by homesteaders from 1902 to 1904, there was considerable friction between the cattlemen and settlers. A free-range law was in force at that time. Under this law it was necessary for a settler to have a legal fence around his field before he could collect any damage to his crops by range cattle. A legal fence was defined as having not less than three well-stretched wires with posts not less than a rod apart and two stays between each post.

All farms had some cattle, generally 30 or 50 head per quarter section (160 acres). By the early 1900s, longhorns had declined and other more manageable and better meat- and milk-producing breeds were the choice. Longhorns were difficult to manage in enclosed fences and could be dangerous to handle in closed spaces, as milking required. About a third of each farm's herd was sold off each year to cattle buyers. These would have been the young bulls and steers (castrated males), grazed to maturity through spring, summer, and fall. Most were fed grain and forage crops during the winter, when the grass had been grazed down or it was snow-covered. Farmers usually kept about half of their farms in grass, and they allowed their cattle to occasionally graze their wheat crop for a short while in the early spring before the wheat headed up, a process that did only minimal damage to the crop.

Milk products were a major source of income for most prairie farms. Immediately after milking, warm fresh milk was run through a hand-cranked cream separator to isolate the butterfat. Wayne Lewis, in a letter to the author, wrote (2002):

There was a tank at the top that would hold several gallons—more than a milk pail. We ran the milk through a strainer with a disposable cloth disk as the milk went into the tank. The faucet from the bottom of the tank fed into a bowl-like thing above the separator. This bowl had a float that automatically controlled the flow of milk. The separator was a cylinder that spun at perhaps 1,000 revolutions a minute. Inside were about 50 disks spaced close together, perhaps 1/50th inch apart and the centrifugal force caused the cream, which was lighter, to concentrate near the center. It exited through openings to the cream spout while the milk escaped through another spout at a ratio of [about] 10:1. The cream was still only 40 percent butterfat.

Soured milk also would clabber and then cheese could be made from the curds that collected at the top and were squeezed in muslin cloth to wring out the fluids. The residual fluids from both of these processes were fed to the hogs on the farm.

The 1902 Sears, Roebuck & Co. catalog (No. 111) contained at least three pages of dairy equipment, including churns, butter workers and molds, cheese making apparatuses, milk testers, milk cans and buckets, and cream separators. From its home office in Chicago,

Sears, Roebuck & Company was a leading supplier of farm goods for rural families all across the Midwest and Great Plains.

Nearly every farm had a cream separator to separate butterfat from milk. Cream separators were dangerous pieces of equipment, usually with exposed gears. Many a child's finger was lost in these gears as they pushed butterfat back down into the separator while the machine operated. Forrest lost a finger and Harold nearly lost one in the Crafts' cream separator.

The advantage of producing cream and cheese for sale was that it concentrated the dairy products, thus lowering the bulk and weight **(Figs. 4.2 and 4.3).** Cheese had a much longer shelf life than raw milk and could be transported farther. Refrigeration of milk and dairy products during travel was a problem, particularly in the summer. The 3.5-mile trip into Gate once or twice a week to take cream, cheese, butter, and possibly some milk presented little problem for the Crafts, as they were able to capitalize on their farm's nearness to town. Farmers living twice as far from the market had more difficulty getting their dairy products—particularly milk—to town on warm days. By 1915-17, the Craft's advantage was diminished by the automobile.

Up until 1920 or so, there was a major market for horses and mules around Gate, as virtually all sources of power on the farms were from horses and mules. Although oxen had played a minor role as a draft animal prior to 1900, within ten years, oxen were seldom used. Horses were often traded both in town and out on the Craft farm. Horse-trading, practiced by nearly all farmers of the time, was a "buyer beware" activity.

Maurie (1995) remembered:

I remember Papa was making a trade deal with somebody with a horse that he had. And Mom said to him, "Did you tell him that he [the horse] was blind in one eye?" Papa said, "No one told me he was blind in one eye when I bought him."

Fig. 4.2. Cream bottle, circa 1912-23, found buried near the location of the "spring house" cooling trough on the Craft farm, 2002. *(Source: Author, 2002)*

From the time the Crafts arrived in Oklahoma in 1904 until they departed in 1924, horses were critical to the operation of the farm. Steam engines were used mostly with the threshing machine. Charley's purchase of the Ford touring car about 1917 or 1918 eased life somewhat, but the horse remained the dominant source of power on the farm.

Fig. 4.3. Lip of cream bottle found on the Craft farm, 2002. *(Source: Author, 2002)*

There is no indication that the Crafts ever had a conventional tractor. So all plowing, cultivating, and hauling on the farm was done using horses as draft animals. Generally, Charley had two draft horses used to pull a turning plow to break the ground for planting in the spring. The horses would then pull a drag harrow over the plowed ground; then wheat seed would be broadcast over the leveled soil. Where corn or other row crops were to be planted, the horses would pull a lister, a double-moldboard plow that threw up ridges separating a deep furrow and planted the seeds as it went along the ridges. This configuration allowed the furrows to trap and hold any moisture and windblown soil particles that moved through the process of *saltation* (being bounced along by the wind). Draft horses were also used at harvest, pulling a wagon into the field to haul crops back to the barn.

Charley also kept one or two horses for riding. The children fondly remembered one such horse named Target. Harold called him "my pony." Both Maurie and Harold spoke of riding Target around the farm, to the swimming hole on Horse Creek, and to school.[63]

Commercial Crops

Wheat was the principal commercial crop grown around Gate. In wet years, wheat would be abundant and its storage was a major problem on farms where outbuildings were few. Even abandoned houses were sometimes used to store grain. Occasionally, the wheat harvest would be so large that surplus wheat simply would be dumped on the ground in the yard or a fenced enclosure.

From 1904 through 1924, the prairie around Gate, Oklahoma, had good crop years and poor ones. About one out of every three years was considered good, although several bad years would often be strung together, creating a lengthy drought. The dry years were very troubling. Harold Craft (1995) particularly remembered the cycles in the late 1910s and early 1920s:

> . . . I know that [when] drought would set in, we weren't able to grow enough crops to feed the livestock. We just didn't have any feed. We weren't able to grow grass. The grain had quit growing because of two reasons. It seems as though the seasons had changed and we had the dust bowl and wheat would blow out of the ground. The rains had quit coming. You just couldn't grow any grain. . . . I remember seeing cattle starved to death. And horses starved to death down there.

The country had actually gone from a land of plenty, really there, because I have seen the times when we didn't have enough places to store all the grain. I have seen grain stacked high. Pigs [would be] running loose and running into . . . wheat and corn that were stacked right on the ground because we didn't have [enough places] or granaries to put the grain.

Up until about 1915, wheat was threshed by a horse-drawn threshing machine, called a separator. Around that year, however, several Gate residents pooled their resources to buy their first steam-driven threshing machine. This was a major purchase, trusted to Charley Craft and John Card.

Charley and his neighbors purchased a new Case steam engine and separator and had it delivered by rail to Alva, Oklahoma. Charley and John rode their horses to Alva to pick up the equipment and drive it back to Gate. This was a huge black steam engine-driven machine with lugged steel wheels and a galvanized separator with a bright red wooden box.

Harold describes (1996) the community efforts to purchase a threshing machine:

My dad and John Card had wheat and wheat crops that you wouldn't believe [the] production. They didn't have any way of threshing it. And absolutely nobody in the area out there had any way of threshing the wheat. But the ones that instigated this—the getting of this thrashing machine—was my dad and John Card. They went to all these farmers that had the wheat and got so much money, enough to buy this steam engine and thrasher-separator. And ordered the machine and had it delivered to the railhead at Alva, Oklahoma. So my dad and John Card went to the railhead and got this steam engine. An old Case steam engine and separator.

The trip across the prairie from Alva to Gate was 73 miles. Choosing not to follow the wagon tracks across the grassland, Charley and John Card struck out due west across the prairie with this lumbering, smoke-belching giant of a machine at a speed of only about two or three miles per hour. Harold's most vivid description (1996) of how Charley and John Card brought the big black and red Case across the prairie produces an exciting and inspiring image:

And they had to drive that thing, as slow as it was, from Alva to Gate. They started out there and, of course, they run out of fuel [wood]. Well, then they run out of steam. So they tied the steering on so it would run straight ahead across the prairie. One of them got on one side and the other one on the other side and they started gathering buffalo chips [cow chips to fuel the steam engine]. Began stoking that thing with buffalo chips in order to furnish steam to run that thing—to keep the steam up, to keep it rolling. The sparks that come out of the chimney of the smokestack set the prairie on fire. So my dad and John Card tried to put out the prairie fire [with their coats], but it got away from them. They set the prairie on fire, but it was such wild country and nobody out here, so they just let the prairie fire go. Went back to [picking up buffalo chips], driving the steam engine and kept on going.

As soon as Charley and John Card arrived with the machinery, they started to work on the harvest. The time of year would have been early to mid-June. Harold (1995) tells what happened when the equipment arrived:

The first thing they started in was they began threshing grain for the farmers that had contributed money to get the steam engine and threshing equipment back [to Gate].

Having a self-powered threshing machine was a distinct advantage for the farmers around Gate. Horse-drawn separators were inefficient. The availability of the Case separator quickly increased the profitability of wheat as a commercial crop.

Describing how the threshing machine worked, Harold (1996) said:

There [was] a header that you had to cut the wheat and stack it in stacks so close together that the separator is pulled between the two wheat stacks. Then you feed the separator from either side. There is one of those separators—no, one of the headers—in the museum in Gate right now.

The result was an increase in efficiency in harvesting, and many farmers increased their wheat acreage. Although moisture was always a major factor in the size of the wheat harvest, the introduction of the steam engine to farming around Gate changed the limiting factors from the time-consuming harvesting process to those of grain storage and transportation.

Wildfires

Of all the storms Beaver County homesteaders had to endure, blizzards may have been the most stressful on humans and their farm animals. Among all of the natural phenomena, however, wildfires and tornadoes were by far the most dangerous. In the first decade of the 20th century, wildfires were extremely worrisome on the open prairie. As more and more of the land was plowed and planted to wheat and other crops, the threat of wildfires diminished somewhat. Nonetheless, under strong winds, wildfires were among the most feared physical phenomena.

From the middle of summer through early fall, the prairie turned brown, as both the buffalo grass and crops would become tender dry and easily burned. Lightning associated with afternoon and evening thundershowers was the usual source of wildfires, although occasionally humans would accidentally set fires. Once a fire began—often out of sight—it could race across the prairie, pushed by the wind.

Farmers generally kept firebreaks of cropland or closely cropped pasture around their farm buildings. When the community was alerted to a wildfire, farmers joined in fighting it with wet burlap bags and even fresh cowhides dragged along the fire line between two horses. Often wildfires were simply uncontrollable because of high wind.

Because they were constructed of wood, barns were usually more susceptible than dugouts or soddies to raging prairie fires. Many homesteaders relinquished their homesteads because a wildfire burned them out— their buildings, crops, and livestock—years of work gone in seconds.

Luckily, the Craft farm was never overrun by a wildfire, to the best of our knowledge, but the community was often threatened, and Charley and the boys, no doubt, helped in such emergencies. It was just one more threat with which the Crafts and other homesteaders lived year after year.

CHAPTER 5

LEAVING THE HOMESTEAD

Finances From 1906-1912

Charley applied for the Oklahoma homestead in 1905, and he and Martha worked to "prove up" on it until they received their Final Receipt Record on 25 August 1910 from the Department of the Interior United States Land Office in Woodward, Oklahoma.[64] This document stated, ". . . that on presentation of this certificate to the Commissioner of the General Land Office, the said Charles V. Craft shall be entitled to a patent for the tract of land above described" (the Craft homestead). Although Charley did not actually apply for his official patent until 26 October 1914, this document provided sufficient proof of ownership to begin borrowing money against the land.

There is no record of the Crafts borrowing any money on the 120-acre homestead from 1905 to 1910. In fact, Charley could not officially place a mortgage on the farm until he had received his Homestead Certificate (of ownership). On the day he received his Certificate, he and Martha mortgaged the farm to Sam'l H. Graves of the First Trust and Savings Bank in Chicago (8 August 1910) for $600 at an annual interest rate of seven percent.

The due date on the note was 1 October 1915.[65] Although the interest was probably paid regularly, this loan wasn't repaid to First Trust until 21 October 1914, after the Crafts returned from Palacios, Texas **(Table 2)**. The preceding dry years in 1908 and 1910 and resulting poor harvests may have precipitated this loan.

TABLE 2
CHARLEY CRAFT'S FINANCIAL DEALINGS
From the Beaver County, OK, Clerk's Office
(Rel) = Mortgage or debt released, or paid off.

#	Grant-or	Grantee	Date. Exec.	Date Rec.	Charac-ter	Book-Pg	Re-marks
1	Land Office	Charles V. Craft	08-08-10	08-25-10	H'stead Certificate		
2	Chas. Craft/wf	Sam'l H. Groves	08-22-10	08-25-10	Mortgage	14-354	$600 (rel #9)
3	U.S. Gov't	Charles V. Craft	03-06-11	10-26-14	Patent	31-336	120 acres
4	WE Pratt/wf	Charles V. Craft	10-07-12	01-09-13	Mortgage	11-612	$2,800 (Rel #8,#11
5	Charles V. Craft	WE Pratt et al.	12-07-12	08-06-17	Warty Dd	42-235	$4,000
6	Charles V. Craft	Pittsburg Mtg Inv. Co.	06-02-14	06-15-14	Mortgage	1-131	$1,000 (Rel #19)
7	Charles V. Craft	Pittsburg Mtg. Inv. Co.	06-02-14	06-15-14	Mortgage	26-98	$140 (Rel #14)
8	Charles Craft	WE Pratt et al (in TX)	06-15-14	06-15-14	Release	Misc-216	$2,800
9	First T&S Bk.	Charles. V. Craft	10-16-14	10-21-14	Release	35-301	$600

10	WE Pratt	Charles V. Craft (TX)	02-14-14	08-06-17	War'ty Dd	42-231	120 acres
11	Charles V. Craft	WE Pratt et al	08-06-17	08-06-17	Release	38-511	$2,800
12	Charles V. Craft	Fed. Land Bank	10-03-17	10-01-17	Mortgage	49-71	$1,600 (Rel)
13	Charles V. Craft	OO Mendenhall	12-15-17	09-04-18	O&G Lease	4-553	
14	Pittsburg Mtg Co.	CV Craft	05-15-18	5-20-18	Release	34-25	$140
15	C.V. Craft	TH? Collins	04-12-20	05-03-20	O&G Lease	5-221	40 acres
16	C.V. Craft	St. Bk of Com. Gate	06-20-22	06-26-22	Mortgage	65-416+	$1,000 (Rel #18)
17	C.V. Craft	St. Bk of Com. Gate	06-16-24	07-09-24	War'ty Dd	52-470	$3,000
18	St. Bk of Com Gate	C.V.Craft	09-05-28	09-08-28	Release	75-477	$1,000
19	Andrew Jarmette, Ex.	C.V. Craft	11-20-28	12-12-28	Release	75-494	$1,000
20	Federal-Land Bank	C.V. Craft	05-28-35	06-26-35	Release	91-200	$1,600

The years between 1905 and 1912 appear to have been mostly good, though difficult years for the Crafts, with at least two of the years being dry (1908 and 1910). The fact that Charley and Martha were able to survive as homesteaders and make a life for their family on their prairie farm without outside support is a credit to both of them and their farming abilities. It is significant, however, that Charley mortgaged the farm for only $600 in 1910, raising the question about the value of the farm at that time. A sum of $600 would have been a great deal of money, but the Craft homestead easily should have been worth more than that.

By 1912, the Craft family had proved up on their farm, built a house and barn on the property, and added fencing. The family had grown to include five children. The 120-acre farm was now worth about $30 to $50 per acre, which could provide a potential grubstake of $3,600 to $6,000 or more, if a buyer was interested.[66]

The Crafts perceived their homestead as a grubstake from the very beginning. The first seven years on the farm had to have been exceedingly difficult as the young family worked to prove up on their homestead, but they persevered. With their growing family, Charley and Martha had to realize that the only long-term future they might have in Gate was to either purchase more land or to sell out. Whether Charley was renting more land at this early stage of the family's living in Gate is questionable, simply because there was relatively little mechanized farm equipment. The Crafts, as a young, struggling family prior to 1912, one without a sizeable bankroll, simply did not see the prospects for buying more land.

The most difficult part of living long-term on a Panhandle homestead was the undependable weather and its effect on farm income. According to Wayne Lewis (2002), only two of every three years were good farming years there. Even into the 1920s, most Panhandle families were living on 50 cents per day.

If, indeed, the Crafts saw their homestead as a grubstake, the winter and summer of 1911-12 may have helped them make up their minds to sell their property.

The cold, snowy winter—clearly the worst they had endured—probably set the stage for one of the farm's best crops the following summer. Heavy snowfall covered the area's winter wheat crop and provided abundant soil moisture into the spring and summer. This may have been even the best wheat crop experienced in the area over the past decade. Up until this time, the Crafts had only borrowed $600 against their farm.

It is difficult to know exactly what drove the Crafts to search for ways to sell or lease the farm. They may have wanted simply to leave the farm after enduring the most difficult winter they had ever experienced. Or, perhaps, after harvesting their best crop ever and having experienced the boom and bust cycles of weather, the Crafts decided that it was the time to sell. Alternatively, they may have received an opportunistic offer for the land. It appears, however, that their intent was to seek a deal that left as many doors open for them as possible, e.g. the option of returning to the farm later or consummating the sale later after they were able to assess some alternatives.

Charley found that he could make a deal on the farm with W.E. Pratt and his wife, Cassia M. Pratt, and A.B. Card in the summer or fall of 1912. The Pratts were from Matagorda County, Texas. A.B. Card, from Gate, was the realtor and land developer who probably arranged the deal and joined as a co-signer.

A.B. Card may have used the fact that the 1912 harvest had been larger than normal as a selling point. He was not above using such marketing techniques to help sell property, as evidenced by one of his promotional photographs of farmers kneeling in an alfalfa field to show the crop as high as their chests.[67] Why Card chose to invest

is still an unanswered question. As a realtor, he would
have wanted to sell the Craft farm at the highest price
possible in order to increase his commission. Moreover,
his co-signing the loan may have been an assurance to the
Pratts that the deal was a good one.

Thus, on 7 December 1912, W.E. Pratt and A.B.
Card signed a "... mortgage agreement which was intended
as a part of the purchase price in a sale of the land . . . to
Pratt . . . and Card by Charles V. Craft. . . ." The purchase
agreement was for $4,000, minus the $600 first mortgage
to Samuel Graves and perhaps $600 cash to Charley. Pratt
and Card promised to make three installments of $933.33
each ($2,800) to Charley and Martha at 6.5% interest.
There is no indication that Charley received any payment
at this time, other than the $600 he received upon the
signing of this document. In fact, the agreement was not
recorded until two years later, on 7 December 1914. This
seems to indicate that neither party was certain about the
ultimate outcome of the deal. From the legal documents
associated with the deed:

> *This indenture, made this 7th day of December A.D.
> 1912 between Charles V. Craft and Martha Craft
> husband and wife of Beaver County in the State
> of Oklahoma, of the first part and W.E. Pratt and
> A.B. Card of the second part: Witnesseth, that said
> parties of the first part, in consideration of the sum
> of Four Thousand and no/100 ($4,000) dollars,
> the receipt whereof is hereby acknowledged, do
> by these presents grant, bargain, sell and convey
> unto the said part(ies) of the second part their
> heirs and assigns all the following described Real
> Estate, situated in the County of Beaver, State*

of Oklahoma, to-wit: (A legal description of the Craft farm follows), Except one first mortgage of $600.00, the same held by Samuel H. Graves of Chicago, drawing interest at the rate of 6 ½%, due Oct. 1st 1915.[68]

The second document was a Mortgage of Real Estate, finalizing the deal. It was signed seven days later on 14 December 1912 in Matagorda County, Texas, and was recorded 9 January 1913 in the Beaver County, Oklahoma, Records Office. Mrs. Pratt had not been in Gate at the time the first paper was drawn up, so she was not able to sign the original note. She had to sign this document as W.E. Pratt's wife, consummating the deal. This document signed in Texas was a note on the Craft farm for the $2,800 to be paid in installments over three years, completing the deal for $4,000 for the Craft farm. The formal document, a Mortgage of Real Estate, concluded the deal.

This Indenture, made this 7th day of Dec. A.D. 1912 between W.E. Pratt & C.M. Pratt (husband and wife) and A.B. Card of Beaver County, in the State of Oklahoma, of the first part, and Charles V. Craft of the second part: WITNESSETH, The said parties of the first part in consideration for the sum of Twenty Eight Hundred & no/100— ($2,800.00)—DOLLARS, the receipt whereof is thereby acknowledged, do by these presents, grant, bargain, sell and convey unto said parties of the second part, his heirs and assigns, all the following described Real Estate, situated in Beaver County, Oklahoma State, to-wit: [A legal description of the Craft farm follows]. One year after [this] date, I, we, or either of us promise to pay to the order of

Charles V. Craft and the State Bank of Commerce, Gate, Oklahoma ## nine hundred thirty-three and 33/100### dollar, with interest at the rate of 6 ½ per cent per annum from date until paid. Value received, interest payable annually. The interest, if not paid annually, to become as principal and bear the same rate of interest; and if this note is not paid when due and the same is placed in the hands of an attorney for collection, or if suit is brought thereon, I, we, or either of us agree to pay an additional amount of the protest and consent that time of payment may be extended from time to time without notice. [Payment] No. 1 due December 7th, 1913. The other two notes are of the same date, one being for $933.33, due December 7th, 1914 and the other one for $933.34, due December 7th, 1915. [69]

Both the original note and the Mortgage of Real Estate agreement are parts of the same deal. The only differences are that W.E. Pratt and A.B. Card signed the first one, while W.E. Pratt, his wife, C.M. Pratt, and A.B. Card signed the second one in Texas. Mrs. Pratt had apparently remained in Texas while her husband had been in Gate making the deal with Charley through realtor A.B. Card. Therefore, it was essential to Charley to add Mrs. Pratt's name to the mortgage there in Texas on 14 December 1912, when he met with the Pratts and A.B. Card at the notary's office in Matagorda County. Mrs. Pratt signed the paperwork without ever seeing the Craft farm, as described below:

Before me, W.H. Brooks, a Notary Public in and for side State [Texas] and County [Matagorda] on this 14th day of December A.D. 1912 personally appeared W.E. Pratt to me known to be the identical person

*who executed the within and foregoing instrument,
and acknowledged to me that he executed the same
as his free and voluntary act and deed for the uses
and purposes therein set forth. In witness whereof
I have hereunto set my and offered my notarial
seal . . . Before me, WH. Brooks in and for said
State and County on the 14ᵗʰ day of December A.D.
1912, personally appeared C.M. Pratt, wife of W.E.
Pratt, to me known to be the identical person who
executed the within and forgoing instrument and
acknowledged that she executed the same as her
free and voluntary act and deed for the uses and
purposes therein set fourth.*[70]

These two documents substantiate the fact that
the Pratts were from Texas and that Charley had made
a deal with them. That A.B. Card, Gate's leading real
estate agent, co-signed the note certainly meant that he
was acquainted with the Pratts and knew something about
their finances before, joining the deal. A.B. Card knew
Charley and Martha, as he was the relative of John Card,
Charley and Martha's close friend.

The Crafts took a $600 cash down payment from
the Pratts and A.B. Card, kept a $600 mortgage to the
bank, and held a note for three payments of $933.33 each,
making the total purchase price close to $4,000. This was a
good price for 120 acres in 1913, considering that Beaver
County, Oklahoma, farmers had one bad year out of every
three. In fact, the Craft farm was one of the poorer ones
around Gate, with more slope and less flat land than most
other homesteads.

Immediately after Charley and Martha signed
the papers to sell their farm on 7 December 1912 and

received $600 in cash, the family left for Palacios, Texas, arriving sometime before 14 December. Charley and Martha left Beaver County believing they had achieved their grubstake and were moving to greener pastures in Palacios, Texas, home of the Pratts.

There is some indication that Charley and Martha may have worked out a more sophisticated land deal with W.E. Pratt and his wife, C.M. Pratt, than just a simple purchase of the Craft's farm in Gate. The fact that the Crafts relocated to precisely the same locality in Texas where the Pratts lived indicates that there may have been considerable communication between the two families before, during, and after the sale of the Craft farm. Perhaps the Pratts assisted in Charley's application for a job on a local dairy in Palacios, Texas. Without knowing much about the Pratts, however, this is speculation based solely upon the coincidences of the relationship.

Life in Texas, 1912-14

Palacios is located on Palacios Bay about midway between Houston and Corpus Christi, requiring the Craft family to take a train trip the length of Texas. They traveled from Perryton, the most northern Texas railhead at the time, to the Gulf Coast, a distance of nearly 750 miles.

According to family's oral history, Charley became a worker on a dairy farm just north of Palacios, Texas.[71] The farm may have been one owned by the Elder family, as that was the largest dairy operational in the area around Palacios at that time.[72] In those days, local dairy farms often bottled and delivered milk to the community.

The only Elder family listed in the 1910 U.S. Census for Palacios was Pearl W. Elder, who had a wife and nine children.[73] His occupation is listed as a cashier at a bank. There is no indication that he ran or owned a dairy in 1910, but he may have owned an interest in it by 1912.

Craft family oral history also indicated that Charley might have received the job through his contacts with the Quakers.[74] There is no record, however, of there being a Quaker church in Palacios between 1912 and 1914. Given the events that followed over those two years, relatives or close friends of the Pratts somehow might have been involved with the dairy on which Charley worked.

According to the 1910 U.S. Census, there was only one W.E. Pratt and family living in Palacios two years before the Crafts arrived. Wilbur E. Pratt, 40 years old, was listed as a hotel agent and his wife's name was Cassarilla (perhaps anglicized to Cassia). She was 27 years old, and they had four children, the oldest of whom was 14 in 1910.[75] It is certain that this was the W.E. Pratt and wife Cassia, who bought the Craft homestead with A.B. Card. As a hotel agent, Wilbur Pratt may have accumulated enough money for the down payment. Why they chose farming or how the contact was made with the Craft family is uncertain, but probably Gate realtor A.B. Card served as the contact with the Crafts. It is also possible that W.E. and Cassia Pratt bought the Craft farm for their oldest son, William, who would have been 17 in 1913. Perhaps their intent was to give William a grubstake. By 1920, the census no longer listed the Pratts in Palacios, Texas, or Gate, Oklahoma. They seem to have disappeared.

Some of this is speculation, as relatively little is known about the Crafts' two years in Texas. There was no Quaker Church and they were not listed as members of the Methodist Church in Palacios.[76] There is also no ready evidence that Charley and Martha purchased any property in Palacios during their stay.

Dairying was something Charley knew, however, having milked cows as a boy on the Doubs' Pfafftown, North Carolina, farm, worked on a local dairy farm in Carmel, Indiana, and handled his own cattle in Gate. The availability of a steady, paying job at a dairy also may have helped entice the Crafts to move to Palacios, after the inconsistent income from the Craft farm.

The Craft family stayed less than two years in Texas, before moving back to Gate and taking over the Craft farm again. Once more, we know little about what influenced them, but it appears that the Pratts defaulted on their loan by missing the first $933.33 payment. A tornado or windstorm had destroyed part of the Craft barn and perhaps some of the Pratts' crops and livestock in Gate during the Crafts' absence. It also appears that 1913 was a dry year and resulted in a poor crop yield. This left the Pratts unable to make their scheduled payment. Faced with losing most of the value of and investment in the farm in Gate, Charley and Martha returned to Oklahoma in 1914.

Charley repurchased the farm in Gate from the Pratts and A.B. Card in February 1914. This buy-back is significant because the Crafts were acknowledging that they were committed to reclaiming their farm. It appears that they could have foreclosed on the farm and actually reclaimed it without buying it back since they held the mortgage and the buyers had defaulted. On the other hand, it may have been that their friend, A.B. Card, was involved in the sale and the Crafts felt indebted to him. Alternatively, perhaps he shamed them into returning the down payment. Regardless, they did the honorable thing in paying back the $600 down payment and released the Pratts' and A.B. Card from the land deal.

> *This indenture, made this 14ᵗʰ day of February A.D. 1914, between W.E. Pratt and Cassia M. Pratt (husband and wife) and A.B. Card (a single man) of Beaver County, in the State of Oklahoma, of the first part, and Charles V. Craft, of the second part: Witnesseth, that said parties of the first part, in consideration of the sum of Four Thousand & no/100 $4,000.00 dollars, the receipt whereof is hereby acknowledged, does by these presents grant, bargain, sell and convey into the said party of the second part, his heirs and assigned all the following described Real Estate, situated in the County of Beaver, State of Oklahoma, to-wit: [followed by a legal description].*[77]

On 1 June 1914 in Matagorda County, Texas, Charley again mortgaged the Craft farm, this time for $1,000 on a first mortgage and $140 on a second mortgage, both to Pittsburg Mortgage Investment Company of Pittsburg, Kansas.[78] By then, Charley had regained ownership, he and Martha were looking ahead, and they realized that they needed some cash to move back to Gate and perhaps even to repair their house and barn upon arrival.

The following day, 2 June 1914, Charley released the Pratts and A.B. Card from the mortgage in a handwritten and signed document recorded in both Matagorda County, Texas, and Beaver County, Oklahoma. This action was probably requested by the Pratts, who wanted to clear up any legal questions about the deal in their home county, as well as in Beaver County, Oklahoma.

In consideration of the payment of the debt named therein, I hereby release the mortgage dated December 7, 1912, and executed by W.E. Pratt and C.M. Pratt his wife, and A.B. Card, mortgagor to Charles V. Craft, mortgager, conveying the following described real estate, situated in Beaver County, State of Oklahoma, to wit: [the farm's legal description follows]. This mortgage was intended as a part of the purchase price in a sale of the land herein described to the said W.E. Pratt and C.M. Pratt and A.B. Card by Charles V. Craft, but said sale was not consumated [sic] and the deed from the said Charles V. Craft was not delivered. Witness my hand this 2nd day of June A.D. 1914. [signed] Charles Craft. [Notarized by] J.J. Harrison, Matagorda County, Texas.[79]

A formal Release of the Mortgage Record was later signed in 1917 and officially recorded in the Beaver County Records Office. This brought legal closure to the land deal between the Pratts, A.B. Card, and the Crafts.

In consideration of the payment of the debt named therein, I hereby release the mortgage dated December 7, 1912 and executed by W.E. Pratt & C.M. Pratt, husband and wife, and A.B. Card, mortgagors to Charles N. Craft, mortgagee, conveying the following describe real estate situated in Beaver County, State of Oklahoma, to-wit: [followed by the legal description]. [80]

This is evidence that the Pratts had failed to make their first crops on the Craft farm. They had not made their first $933.33 payment to the Crafts in 1913 and perhaps initially even asked Charley to carry the first year's payment over. It may have been such a devastating year for the Pratts on the Craft farm, however, that they were not willing to chance another year. If there were family ties between the Pratts and the owner of the dairy in Palacios, that may have further pressured Charley and Martha to settle with the Pratts.

The Craft family had to return to Gate and pick up the pieces at the farm or lose the hard-won grubstake. This would certainly have been very disappointing to Charley and Martha, both of whom surely thought they had made a firm, honorable, and successful deal with the Pratts nearly two years prior.

Charley and Martha had some money at their discretion and felt the need to pay off the $600 loan on their farm in Gate made back in 1910. On 21 October 1914, after they left Texas, Charley paid off the loan to Sam'l H. Graves and First Trust & Savings Bank of Chicago. The Crafts may have wanted to clear the deed to their farm in order to make a fresh start, although the loan was not scheduled to be repaid until 7 October 1915. Perhaps the money to pay the loan came from Charley's work on the dairy farm. Nothing in the documents in the Beaver County Records Office sheds any light on this.

Martha was pregnant with Forrest in the summer of 1914, and despite her pregnancy, the family returned to Gate during the early fall, probably in September. The family arrived by train at Perryton, Texas, with all of their household belongings and their five children. Perryton, the closest railhead in Texas, was located about 10 miles south of the Oklahoma line and about 75 road miles from Gate. Charley arrived in Perryton by train more than a week earlier, went on to Gate, and borrowed a team of horses and a wagon from his neighbors.[81] He drove the team back (about 20 to 35 miles per day), picked up the family and all of the household goods, and struck out across the prairie for Gate again. The entire one-way trip by wagon would have taken two or three days, during which time Martha had to care for the five children. The oldest boy, Paul, at 16 years of age, and Buelah (11) would have been able to help on the long trip with the three younger children, Maurie (7), Cecil (5), and Harold (2).

As they loaded the wagon at the railhead, two-year old Harold Craft was startled by the steam engine as it let off steam in the yard, probably also scaring the horses which had never experienced the sound before. This was the first thing Harold remembered in his life, as he described:

I was born in 1912, but I have no remembrance of moving to Texas and very little of living in Texas because we moved back sometime late in, I would guess, 1913 [actually 1914]. That's after my dad had sold the farm and had moved to Texas. My dad ran a dairy in Corpus Christi [actually, Palacios], Texas, and then the fellow who had bought the farm in Gate had defaulted on the payment on it. Among the reasons was the fact [that] there had

*been a tornado that had blown the barn away. So
we moved back to Gate and settled there again . .
. the closest rail line we could get was Perryton,
Texas. When we come back [from] Corpus Christi,
we unloaded everything at Perryton. . . . Pa had
come ahead and had gotten a wagon and horses.
Borrowed this team of horses and wagon in Gate
and had driven from Gate south to Perryton . . .
and picked up me and the folks at the railroad. . . .
We drove across the prairie to Gate and settled in
the dugout that my dad had originally set up to live
in there in Gate. I do remember getting a scare at
the railroad [when] the engine let off steam. And
that is probably the only thing I remember that
whole trip.*[82]

A more recent Perryton train station stands today
just a few yards east of the original station. The track
runs along the crest of a terrace just north of Perryton and
the station sits on the south side of the track, only about
a block or two from the center of town. Unloading the
family's goods from the train and onto the wagon must
have been a cheerless job for the family in the early fall
of 1914, knowing that their attempt to sell the farm had
failed and there was yet more than a two-day journey by
wagon to get back to the homestead in Gate.

That trip must have been particularly excruciating
for Martha in the last months of her pregnancy. She rode in
the farm wagon, which had no springs, over rutted wagon
roads and open prairie between Perryton and Gate. The
family probably slept in or under the wagon at night.

117

CHAPTER 6

BACK TO THE HOMESTEAD

The Craft Family Back in Gate, 1914

When the Craft family returned to Gate, the Pratts had already departed. Charley's family moved back into the bank house that Charley had built nine years before and the family settled once more into the rhythms of farming the prairie soils. One of the first things Charley had to do was to get his wheat crop planted and rebuild the barn, which was destroyed by a tornado.[83]

As Charley was repairing the barn in November, Martha began experiencing labor pains. When she told Charley, he asked whether she could hold off a little longer until he could finish the barn. She informed him, clearly, that this was out of her hands.[84] Forrest was born on 13 November at their home in Gate.

The prairie around Gate did not set well with Martha, perhaps even less now than in the early years on the homestead. Coming from a fairly well-heeled Quaker family in Indiana, she never really enjoyed the rigors of life in Gate, particularly the second time around. However, she truly enjoyed the people in the community. Harold fondly remembered:[85]

It was rough living, [but] she [Martha] enjoyed the people [the neighbors] around Gate. They were a wonderful bunch of people. A lot of them were Quakers or Methodists and there were some Presbyterians out there, but they were fine people for the most part—hard working, God-fearing people, and the finest of fine people. They were just the salt of the universe. The people from Indiana that my folks came out with were just great people.

Martha found the uncertainties and hardships of prairie farm life particularly difficult. Other than an occasional cottonwood tree, the rolling, nearly treeless prairie in 1914 was a foreign landscape to a Midwestern woman.

Not even the harsh homestead living, however, could overcome Martha's long and deep interest in music, dating back to her adolescent days in Indiana. Music was one of her greatest pleasures out on the prairie, perhaps because of her father's strict corporal punishment inflicted on her as an adolescent. Harold and Velma Craft and Maurie Craft Lang recalled:

[Mom] raised turkeys and bought a piano with the money . . . and gave lessons to Maurie and Buelah. Mother had a distant cousin or relative that was quite a musician that lived closer to Gate than we did. And [the cousin] did give Maurie and Buelah music lessons. They learned to play the piano. [The piano] was upstairs in one of [our] bedrooms. But Mom always felt like if you didn't have a piano in the house, you didn't have a house. Music was just her thing.[86]

120

In an effort to obtain scarce fruits, Martha's relatives in Indiana shipped peach trees to Gate and Martha had the boys plant them near the well where they could be watered. The trees bore occasional fruit, but early frosts and freezes made their harvests problematic most years.

Dust storms were particularly distasteful to Martha, who helped the children shake the dust out the bedclothes daily during windy periods. Dust seemed to infiltrate everything, even making the food taste gritty at times. During windy periods, dust came in around doors and windows, and it was tracked in by people from the outside. This was very distasteful for a person accustomed to clean clothes and dustless furniture and fixtures.

The daily labors on the farm also were trying, and they aged Martha. The canning, washing, and cooking, punctuated by running the household while Charley and the boys were in the fields or on trips to sell goods or purchase equipment, were anything but monotonous. Martha's postcards and letters, however, were bright and cheery to her mother, her sister Emma, to other family members, and to Della Craft Lineback, Charley's half-sister in North Carolina.

The Craft Family Finances, 1914-24

The Craft's finances were in disarray when they returned to Gate from Texas. They had left Oklahoma in 1912 owing only $600 to a Chicago bank and they were able to pay that off just after returning to Gate in December 1914. The sale of the farm in Gate netted the family nothing in the long run. In fact, the family's moves to Texas and back had cost Charley and Martha a considerable amount. In anticipation of the move from Palacios to Gate to settle on their homestead again, they had borrowed $1,140 on two notes. Hence, the family arrived back in Gate probably with less than $1,000 in cash, and that was mostly borrowed money.

The years following their return in 1914 were moderately good for the most part. Charley and Martha were initially unable to pay off their loans from Pittsburg Mortgage Investment Company in Kansas. In fact, they borrowed $1,600 from the Federal Land Bank on 3 October 1917 and then paid off the $140 note to Pittsburg Mortgage Investment Company on 5 June 1918. The years 1915, 1917, 1918, 1919, 1921, 1922, and 1923 were normal or wet years, apparently allowing Charley and Martha to buy a 1917 Ford touring car for less than $1,000. The fact that they were able to pay off one of their small loans, but neither of the two large loans, one for $1,000 and the other for $1,600, may indicate a series of modest harvests over the period leading up to 1920, which was a particularly dry year.

Oil fever began sweeping Beaver County in 1917, and Charley signed two oil and gas leases on the farm, in hopes that the family might profit from a discovery. He signed one on 15 December 1917 with O.O. Mendenhall and the other on 12 April 1920 with T.H. Collins. The first lease was on the NW ¼ of the SE ¼ and the second on the NW ¼ of the SW ¼ of Section 15, the latter being the 40 acres on which the Craft house and barn were located. Both leases were for $1.00 and were typical five-year oil and gas leases, whereby the lessee agreed to pay the lessor (Charley) if a well on his property produced oil or gas.

Neither gas nor oil was found when a nearby exploratory well was drilled in 1920. The lease became null and void two years later.

Wayne Lewis described the excitement and outcome of the efforts to bring in oil and gas wells around Gate:[87]

> *In 1920, they thought they would strike oil around here [Gate] and they drilled a well. [Drillers] were going to drill 3,000 feet and they were going to shoot the well with nitroglycerin and bring it in. The town was full of cars—hundreds of cars. Hundreds of people came to watch them shoot the well. And nothing happened. Everybody went home. They didn't do any more about oil [around Gate] until the end of the 1940s. So now there is a [gas] well on practically every section.*

On 20 June 1922, Charley borrowed another $1,000, this time from the State Bank of Commerce, Gate. Family oral history frequently suggests that the period leading up to 1922 may have been poor or only marginal crop years.[88] Certainly, the 1920 harvest should have been a poor one since it was a dry year and 1921 was a normal year. It was not until 1922 that the years became wet again, continuing through 1923 and 1924. There may have been other personal reasons that the Crafts needed additional money, necessitating Charley and Martha taking out another loan. The Crafts, however, were unable to repay this loan until 1928, four years after leaving Oklahoma.

By 1922, the Crafts were $3,600 in debt to three different banks. Only nine years before in Palacios,

Texas, they were essentially debt-free. By 1924, two of the children, Paul and Buelah, had graduated from the Laurence Friends Academy; Paul was away in military service and Buelah was teaching part-time locally. Maurie was attending the Academy, and Cecil, Harold, and Forrest were attending middle and elementary school. So there were expenses involved in making sure the children received an education.

The Craft Family and Its Social Ties

During their second tour in Gate, the Crafts were able to overcome some of the hardships on the farm. The family and community had matured, the weather seems to have cooperated somewhat, and the children remembered it as some of the best times in their lives. Harold (1995) thought his life on the homestead was idyllic:

> *I am sure as far as [us] growing up is concerned, it was tough, but we didn't know what we were missing. Looking back on it, why, I think we got in on a lot of stuff that the children nowadays growing up aren't [able to experience]. I think they would be better off growing up like we did.*

Dr. Archie L. Dougan (*doo-GAN*) was Gate's only physician between 1913 and about 1920. He was one of Charley Craft's closest friends, and he played a central role in the Craft family's lives after their return to Gate. Dr. Dougan was born in Randolph County, North Carolina. His father was an Osage doctor (working with the Osage Indians), and Dr. Archie Dougan graduated from the Kansas City Medical College.[89] Harold (1996) summarized what he knew about Dr. Dougan's early life:

> *Archie decided he wanted to become a doctor before his grade schooling was finished. He took the teacher's examination and taught at Randolph County, North Carolina. That was his connection (to North Carolina and Charley) right there. Now why did he go back there? He also returned and taught at the Osage (Indian) School, attended then Trinity and Guilford Colleges in Greensboro, North Carolina. Archie L.—that would have been the one (Dr. Dougan)—was one of the graduates in 1897. That way he probably worked then for 30 years after that. He would have trained, as I understand it, out to western Kansas and then come from Kansas to Oklahoma.*

Everybody respected Dr. Dougan, who served as the only physician within at least a 40-mile radius of Gate up until about 1920. Harold noted: [90]

> *His practice consisted largely of babies, gunshot wounds, and accidents. In 1897 [in Kansas], he did an appendectomy on the kitchen table with a kerosene lantern in a soddy. He came into the territory [Cimarron Territory] in 1904 and got rid of his Englewood property and moved to Beaver County. Apparently, he was trying to give up his practice and just become a farmer. [People] knocked on his doors all hours of the night and day and he just couldn't give up his practice once they found out that he was a doctor.*

Dr. Dougan lived north of Gate and had his own farm, where he and his wife maintained residence. She often served as a nurse and druggist, having learned much about medicine from her husband. She tended the farm, including a small zoo of exotic animals that even included a bear, while Dr. Dougan made house calls. Up until about 1915, all of his house calls were made in a horse and buggy, but about that time, he bought a car, according to Wayne Lewis (2002).

Other than their North Carolina connection, it is unclear why Charley and Dr. Dougan became close friends. The Craft family believed that the friendship was close enough that Charley and Dr. Dougan could confide in one another, according to Harold (1985):

> *He was a great ole guy, I can tell you that. I remember when Dad was sick one time and just feeling so awful bad, laying in bed. Been in bed for what seems to me like two weeks. I don't know how long my dad had been in bed. The doctor came by and tied his horse outside. Come by and sat down in the chair [by the bed] and sat there and visited with my dad. I remember my dad saying, "Doc, you come by all of the time and get up and walk out, never saying anything." He said, "You don't know, you never have looked me over good. You don't know what's a matter with me. How are you going to get me well? You don't know what's wrong with me." I remember Doc reaching over and reaching under the covers and touching my dad and giving him a jab in the side. My dad let out a scream that would raise the roof, you know. "So I don't know what's wrong with you, Charley," he said. "Okay, Doc, you go on home," Dad said. So*

Doc put his hat on and walked on out the door. I don't know if Dad had gallstones or what, but Doc sure hit him in the right place just the same.

Harold Craft continued:[91]

Apparently, Dr. Dougan had a knack for improvising solutions to health problems. An example described in a History of Beaver County [1971] involved Dr. Dougan's own son's [Mike's] health problems at birth. The book describes a baby that was born prematurely, they wrapped him up and laid him down by the stove—wrapped him up in a bundle. After a while somebody happened to look over at him and said, "That little devil wants to live." Dr. Dougan got a box and put some cotton in it and put it in the stove [oven]. He got it hot and put the baby in it, wrapped him up with some water bottles around him and left him. Then they found out the baby's arm had been broken during birth. Someone said, "I'm afraid you are just delaying the inevitable." The doctor gathered up some cardboard from a box and dampened it. With a needle and thread, he sewed the hand and elbow and shoulder inside and fashioned a cast and splint attached to a band around the baby's body. They used the oven to keep him warm. The baby grew up to become Dr. Archie P. [Dougan], but they affectionately called him Mike. He became an eye doctor.

John Card and his family maintained a close relationship and geographical proximity to Charley Craft's family throughout the years. There was a deep respect between the two men and a close social relationship between the families.

Jeanne Carpenter Baker affectionately described her beliefs about Charley and John Card: [92]

> *I have always said that my grandfather [Charley] must have been a real charismatic man. He attracted people. People loved him. Because of the example is John Card. He [John Card] followed him [Charley from Indiana] to Oklahoma; he followed him to Palacios, Texas. He had a family. It wasn't as though he was single. He followed [Charley] back from Oklahoma and from there out to Colorado.*

The Craft family seldom went on true vacations away from Gate. They socialized with other families around Gate Lake where they would picnic and fish for catfish in the two nearby shallow lakes (Gate and Dishpan lakes) when they contained water. Social gatherings often occurred at the Laurence Friends Academy, usually on Saturdays.[93]

Occasionally, the Crafts were able to travel some distances from Gate, but it was usually for a purpose other than vacation. We know that Martha took Buelah and Maurie to Indiana in 1909 on a train almost exactly one year after her father's funeral. The purpose of the trip was probably to settle her father's estate. Buelah would have been six years old and Maurie only two. Martha may have waited a while after her father's death (6 February 1908) to visit Carmel, but her father's death and his estate settlement made the trip necessary at this time. Martha wrote a postcard to Paul just before she, Buelah, and Maurie reached Chicago (3 February 1909).[94]

> . . . *train slow, children tired, leaving for Chicago tonight at 10:15 and get to Indianapolis Wednesday night or by early morning. Hope all is well. [Signed] Momma*

She wrote a second card a few days later (date obliterated):[95]

> *Buelah says to tell you we are homesick.*

Train travel was tiresome in the early 1900s, particularly with children. It is doubtful that the Crafts could have afforded a sleeper car, so the two-day trip would have been by coach from Englewood, Kansas, to Indianapolis, Indiana. The Craft children at this age would not have been very good travelers, perhaps making the Craft farm's quiet setting seem more appealing to both Martha and Buelah. With travel both expensive and tiresome with young children, it is easy to see why the Crafts stayed close to home.

There were nearby recreational opportunities that the Crafts remembered. The Craft children often played in the stock tank (a pond next to the well for watering livestock) at the house. It was fed by the windmill and provided a cool refreshing respite on the farm. Harold and Maurie later said that Charley and Martha encouraged Forrest and Harold to swim in the shallow stock tank—sometimes joined by Cecil—instead of going to the deeper swimming hole on Horse Creek. The swimming hole, sometimes called "the spring," was located about three-quarters of a mile downhill and northwest of the Craft farm. It was a favorite place for the community's older boys to gather on Saturdays. Located at the bottom of a steep undercut bank, the hole was six or seven feet deep, about 20 feet across and perhaps spring fed. It was where many boys learned to swim, as it was smaller and was less dangerous than Gate Lake. The swimming hole on Horse Creek was less intermittent and much safer than the larger Gate Lake. Nonetheless, it was considered too dangerous for the younger children. Consequently, Harold (1995) said that he never learned to swim, in part, because he thought his folks forbade his going to the swimming hole.

All was not idyllic in the Gate Community, however, as social afflictions affected a segment of its society, as is still true of society as a whole. Alleged alcohol abuse and theft were two problems that not only concerned most residents, but also provided fuel for rumor mills and stories passed down for generations. Not only did the Craft adults remember them nearly seventy years later, but also this author heard variations of them in Gate in 2002. Maurie (1995) remembered the antics of one neighbor:

> He [H.O. Henekey] was a drunkard, but a good neighbor. Well, you know as much as Mom was against whiskey and that business, our neighbor to the north, H.O. Henekey . . . he would go into town and get tight and be tight by the time he would come by our house. He'd come by and, of course, he'd begin to get a little sobered up by the time he'd get to the house and he'd call Pop out and talk to him. And he was the one that [told Charley] that they [friends and neighbors] were

*giving the big [surprise] party before we moved—
a going-away party. And so everybody in town
knew it, you know. But he was the one [who told
Charley and ruined the surprise]. Pop never did
tell it [that he knew] until [people started showing
up]. [H.O. Henekey] knew better than [to bring
whiskey to our house].*

Maurie's description brought another from Harold
(1995):

*You know, the early days when these cars, Model
T's come out, they used to sell a hard rubber tire
deal for them. If you want[ed] to repair those
tires, they [the repair items] come in sections of
hard rubber that you could do a home repair job.
When you wore out the tires, you could stuff them
with hard rubber about four inches long. You'd
stuff them down in those 33 X 6 tires. . . . They
would [be] hunks of rubber a little bigger than
your fist. H.O. Henekey was coming home drunk
one night, I remember. Driving that Model T Ford
past our house from Gate up to his house. He had
to drive right in front of our place. And he was
driving along there and the tire had worn out
completely to where those things was a-coming
out of that tire ever once in a while. Every time
one of them would fly out of there [and] hit the
fender of that car and fly out into the air, H.O.
would holler, "Whoopee." Another one would fly
out and . . . he would holler, "Whoopee!"*

Of course, Quakers did not generally consume alcohol. All of the family knew that Martha did not allow it in the house, but both she and Charley appeared to be tolerant of its use elsewhere.

Theft was another matter, however. There was one person in the neighborhood who was regularly accused of petty (and some grand) thievery. Marion Dougherty, who lived across the section road, just west of the Crafts, had a reputation for taking advantage of opportunities. Harold (1995) remembered an episode involving the neighbor:

> *Well, there was a fellow had some cattle up in the pasture just north [of the Craft farm] and one of the cows got down [on the ground]. This fellow was taking oil cake and other feed over to this cow and she was getting better. The cow was in the pasture right across the fence from Marion Dougherty's house. [The owner] fed the cow and [took care of her]. Planned on her getting up the next day, you see, back on her feet. [When he returned the next day, the owner] found [only] the carcass. Just laying there without the skin. So, of course, he knew what had happened to her. Everybody did. So he just headed for Gate and asked the guy who bought hides, "Marion sell you a hide yesterday?" "Yes, as a matter of fact he did," [was the reply]. [The owner] described [the hide] with the spots to [the buyer], etc. "Well," [the buyer] said, "let's roll it out and see what it looks like." He rolled it out and [the farmer] said, "That's my hide. That's it." See, [the cow] was sick and down. [Marion] just went over and saw that she was getting better, going to get up and going to live. So he saw the chance to get that*

hide. So he went over there, killed her, skinned her, and took the hide. I don't know whether [he was] mean, ornery, or just what. I'm just telling you [what apparently happened].

Such stories were spread throughout the close-knit society around Gate. Seldom were such petty perpetrators prosecuted, however, even when the loss was substantial. The farmers preferred to handle it in their own ways and, very often, the results became part of the folk history of the area. Marion Dougherty was the subject of many of Harold's stories (1995):

He [Marion Dougherty] stole stuff, not only from us, but the rest of them [the neighbors]. He got caught all of the time. Everybody was scared to do anything about it [for fear of retribution]. He was a close neighbor. One time one of those floods came by and [our neighbor to the north] [H.O.] Henekey [had] an old sow and about eight or ten pigs, you know. Up north of us this flood came by. These floods come past our house and made a circle through our garden. While it was flooding, that sow come washing down there with her pigs. We watched [them] come by and washed on down over there to Marion's [place]. Of course, when they got down there, they were right by his house—right there [where the draw joins] Horse Creek. Anything got down that far never got any further. He [Marion] had himself a " silent pig." [He killed it.]

Maurie (1995) chimed in:

Almighty Providence was bringing him dinner.

Another case involved Marion Dougherty and a neighbor's wheat.[96]

> . . . the people who lived on the same section we did on the southeast corner of the section was going home from town late one night—[the] Esther Lowes. [They] were going home one night and saw somebody at this particular place [an old house Lowe was using] to store grain. There were no [grain] elevators, so they would take a house that had been vacant like that. They would go in and board up the windows and then fill it with grain— wheat. So [Esther Lowe] was storing wheat in there, awaiting for a better market. So as he was going home, he noticed that there was a wagon backed up to this particular farm building. So he knew that was wrong . . . he went home [and came back]. He . . . watched [at a distance] until that wagon got loaded and pulled out with the wheat. Took off for Englewood, Kansas. [Lowe] followed it a long distance behind to Englewood [and] the elevator. [The thief] sold that load of wheat. When he got it unloaded and went in to draw his check. Mr. Lowe, who owned the wheat, stepped up and said, "I'll take that check." [Marion] Dougherty just backed up and let him have [the check].

Overall, the Gate community was a solid, integrated whole. Quakers, Methodists, and "a few Presbyterians" got along very well, particularly in the early days. Everybody had a tight budget, but most worked very hard for a living on their farms. Helping each other during sickness and at planting and harvesting times was "the thing to do." Sharing farm equipment was common, as was the case of buying the steam engine and threshing machine. Neighbors commonly borrowed equipment from one another, as most could not afford a full complement of horse- or tractor-drawn implements. This borrowing and sharing of equipment helped link the community together and encouraged neighbors to overlook some of the milder transgressions that occasionally affected the population. Interdependency was particularly important when so many had so little.

The Aftermath of Junius Craft's Death

Junius Irving Craft, Charley's father, died in the Craft home in North Carolina on 28 July 1918 at 76 years of age. He had been a Confederate soldier, a small businessman, a farmer, and Methodist Sunday School teacher. The first twenty-nine years of his life had included the stressful events of being shot in the war, the death of his first wife, Harriet Jane Kimel, and giving up his first-born, Charley, in a bound boy situation. Life began to improve for him, however, after he married his second wife, Martha Antonette Styers, on 23 September 1872, almost two years after Charley's birth.

There is the possibility that both Junius and Martha traveled to Indianapolis by rail to visit Charley and Martha around 1900 just prior to Charley's leaving for Oklahoma. The only evidence of this possibility is the name and address of the photographer, *A. Brown, 72 ½ E. Washington St., Indianapolis*, found on a photograph of Junius **(Fig. 6.1)**. His age appears to have been about 58 to 60 years at the time of the photograph.

During the last ten or so years of Junius's life from about 1908 until 1918, he farmed and kept a few cows, two horses, and a little black mule. He commonly rode the mule to Mt. Tabor Church, slightly over a mile toward Winston-Salem on Brookstown Road, where he taught Sunday school. Fondly called "Old Man June" by the neighbors, he was a striking sight with his black suit and long white beard and with a Bible under his arm as he rode to church.

In the last years of his life, his eyesight was failing rapidly. His Lineback grandsons often joked with and played pranks on him, but he enjoyed it. Once when he tied his mule up during church, Jasper (Jack) Lineback turned Junius's saddle around on his mule. After church, Junius untied his little mule and proceeded to mount backwards, a prank enjoyed by everybody, including Junius.[97] This and similar episodes demonstrate Junius's good nature. It also helps us better understand Junius's personality, even after enduring the Civil War.

Neighbors remembered that Junius also sawed up fallen timber on his place and sold it in town during the fall and winter.[98]

Junius and Martha raised five girls and one boy from their marriage, all achieving adulthood on the North Carolina Craft farm **(Fig. 6.2)**. Because he married the second time rather late in life, the last of his children, Blanche, born in 1891, did not move out of the house until about 1909, when Junius was 67 years old. None of the children scattered very far from the Craft home, and all lived around Winston-Salem. At least three lived out their entire lives within a mile of the Craft home. Samuel Irving Craft, the only surviving boy of Junius and Martha's union, was the pride and joy of his family. Consequently, neighbors and relatives often spoke of his being "spoiled" in a family with five sisters.

Fig. 6.1. A tintype of Junius Craft, Charley Craft's father, taken in Indianapolis, Indiana, circa 1902. This is the only circumstantial evidence that Junius might have visited Charley and Martha in Indiana. Because there is a similar photograph of Martha Antionette Styers, Junius's second wife, we might speculate that they both might have traveled by train to Indianapolis. Junius would have been about 60 years of age at this time. *(Source: Permission by Paul Wilburn Jones.)*

Charley was in Gate, Oklahoma, when he heard the news that his father had died. In 1918, it would have been impossible to get to North Carolina in time for the funeral. It is doubtful that Charley contemplated making the trip at this point, although he did come to

North Carolina later.[99] It was also likely that Charley never considered himself very close to his father, having spent little if any time at all in the Craft house prior to leaving for Indiana. We have little evidence of much correspondence between Charley and his father when Charley was in either Indiana or Oklahoma. Charley did ask his father to help him sell the Doub 12 in 1902. Thus, we cannot rule out the possibility that they corresponded, at least through intermediaries. There was probably some second-hand news passed from the Linebacks to Junius from the occasional postcards from Charley's son Paul when the family was in Oklahoma and Texas.

Martha Styers Craft **(Fig. 6.3)** survived Junius by almost five more years, passing away on 26 April 1923. Typically, in the early part of the 20th century, upon the death of the male head of household without a will, his land and property would be divided among his heirs. The wife and each child of his/her surviving family would receive a proportional part of the estate.

An interesting thing happened only twenty-six days before Junius died (2 July 1918), which created a debate among members of the North Carolina Craft and Leinbach/Lineback families persisting to this date. Junius and Martha signed a deed transferring 15.4 acres of their "home place" to their son Samuel for the sum of $1.00 (a common language which may have helped reduce taxes on land transactions).[100]

This deed, made this 2nd day of July, A.D. 1918 by Junius I. Craft and wife, Martha A. Craft, of Forsyth County and State of North Carolina, of the first part, to Samuel I. Craft, of Forsyth County and State of North Carolina, of the second part:

Witnesseth, that the said parties of the first part, in consideration of his legicy [sic] in their real estate and one.00/000 Dollars, to them paid by the said party of the second part, the receipt of which is hereby acknowledged, have bargained and sold, and by these presents do bargain, sell and convey to said party of the second part, and his heirs, all the right, title, interest and estate of the party of the first part in and to tract, or parcel of land in Forsyth County State of North Carolina, adjoining the lands of James E. Pfaff, E.A. Lineback and others, bounded as follows: [A legal property description followed].

The tract of land lay on both sides of Brookstown Road from the Craft house and adjoined Ellis and Della Lineback's property on the east and south. Hiatt Lineback later acquired the adjoining property to the south of this tract from his father Ellis **(Fig. 6.4)**.

Fig. 6.2. The North Carolina Crafts, circa 1940. Left to right, front row: Uncle John Tillet Craft and wife; back row: Charley Craft's halfbrother and -sisters, Odella Craft Lineback, Etta Craft Leinbach, Sam Craft, Virginia Craft Robertson, Daisy Craft Ensley, and Blanche Craft Livingood. *(Source: Permission by Paul Wilburn Jones)*

The purchase of this tract of land by Sam from Junius raised several questions among Junius's surviving children and grandchildren and, in fact, brought considerable criticism down on Sam. Although it is questionable whether the family knew the exact circumstances under which Sam received the deed to the property, most of them believed that Sam had taken advantage of Junius's illness at the time. It is possible, however, that Junius wanted Sam to have a place to build his own house across the road from and adjacent to the old Craft home. It is also possible that Sam convinced his father, who was apparently on his deathbed, to sign the property over to him. The Linebacks believed the latter scenario because in the last year of his life, Junius had to have almost constant care and his faculties were failing him. Carl Sapp (2002) remembered Junius (June) Craft at age 79 and that Carl's brother Harv had taken care of Junius in his last days.[101]

Following Junius's death, the rest of the property was divided, with Martha, each of the daughters, and Sam receiving their portions. There was some question in the family about Charley's portion, as the family was confused about where Charley's portion was located or whether he ever actually gained title to any inheritance.

The questions among the Crafts and Linebacks regarding all of these transactions were "Where was Charley's portion of Junius's estate? Did Junius intend to leave Charley out of his estate? And since there wasn't a will, was Charley not legally entitled to a share of his father's property?" Most thought Charley's portion was supposed to be the tract of land that Junius signed over to Sam just before Junius's death. Throughout the years, these questions were continuously raised by Junius's sisters, daughters, and grandchildren, including sister Senia, daughters Della, Etta, Daisy, and Blanche, and numerous grandchildren: Eula, June, Haywood, Jasper, Hiatt, and Frank Lineback, among others. The answers to the questions, however, remained speculation, many of the family members believing to their deaths that Sam cheated Charley out of his birthright.

Fig. 6.3. Martha Ann Styers, Junius Craft's second wife and Charley Craft's stepmother, circa 1900. *(Source: Permission of Paul Wilburn Jones)*

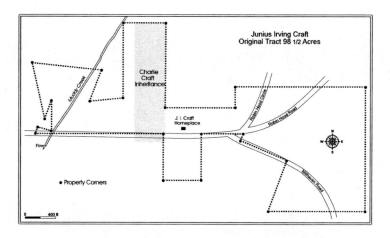

Fig. 6.4. The Junius Craft Place

Charley's Trip to North Carolina, 1922

Sometime between the death of his father, Junius, in 1918, and that of his stepmother, Martha Styers Craft, in 1923, Charley visited North Carolina, probably in 1922. This was the only time he had visited since leaving North Carolina for Indiana the second time in 1890. The actual purposes of this trip are not fully known, but we may speculate on several very interesting issues for Charley that previously were unresolved in North Carolina.

By 1917 or 1918, Charley and Martha had bought a 1917 Ford touring car. This was an open vehicle, whose dependability on a lengthy trip would have been questionable. The odyssey from Gate to Winston-Salem would have been more than 2,400 miles round trip, considerably less than half of which would have been on paved roads in 1922. It is unlikely that Charley would have driven his car on such a long trip.

142

This trip also would have been expensive for Charley to undertake by himself regardless of the mode of transportation. It is unclear whether Charley went by automobile or by train, and none of the family remembered. Members of the Craft family remembered that Dr. Archie Dougan joined Charley on the trip. Dr. Dougan had become one of Charley's closest friends and both men were originally from nearby counties in North Carolina.[102]

If they traveled by auto, the car would more than likely been Dr. Dougan's rather than Charley's. Dr. Dougan knew a great deal more about driving and repairing cars than did Charley, as he had owned a car longer, perhaps as early as 1915.[103]

If they came to North Carolina by train, they probably would have come through Chicago to Winston-Salem. Dr. Dougan had been raised in Randolph County, adjacent to Forsyth County on the southeast and less than 20 miles from the Junius Craft's and Ellis Lineback's houses on Brookstown Road.

By train, it would have taken three or more days each way. By road, the time would have been at least four to six days averaging 200 to 300 miles per day, a standard of daily travel for this period of motor conveyance. If Dr. Dougan and Charley drove, they would most likely have traveled U.S. Highways 64 or 70 across Arkansas, Tennessee, and North Carolina. Highway 64 would have gone through Charlotte, 100 miles from Winston-Salem, while Highway 70 would have passed through Salisbury, 50 miles south. Either would have been possible choices.

Assuming they were driving Dr. Dougan's car, he would have dropped Charley off at Winston-Salem before the short trip to Randolph County.

Charley would not have taken a trip of this magnitude and cost lightly. The Craft family's budget had only recently allowed them to buy their own Ford touring car, but their initial attempt to sell the homestead in Gate had failed, and they were falling deeper and deeper into debt.

In fact, Charley borrowed $1,000 on the farm from State Bank of Commerce, Gate, on 20 June 1922. Speculation is that that money was borrowed *after* his trip to North Carolina and perhaps in anticipation of receiving some inheritance from Junius Craft's estate. In all likelihood, Charley and Dr. Dougan made their trip in January or February 1922. This would have been after the wheat was planted in the fall and before any spring crops were planted. If the trip were made in February, that is even more reason to believe the mode of travel would have been a train rather than a car. Winter travel would have been considerably more problematic by car for that distance at that time of the year.

Regardless of whether they drove a car or rode the train, it is more likely that Charley initiated the trip, rather than Dr. Dougan. We have no idea of the reason Dr. Dougan had for visiting North Carolina, except that he may have had family still in Randolph County. He certainly would have had friends from his years of going to school and teaching there. If it was Charley's trip, it provided an opportunity for Dr. Dougan to go along. In all likelihood, Charley wanted someone with considerable respect in Beaver County, Oklahoma, to accompany him.

Charley probably had some trepidation about this visit, given his adolescent and teenage experiences in North Carolina. Being accompanied by the community's most respected physician would eliminate the possibility of any rumors among the Quakers about the purposes or outcomes of the trip.

It was likely that Charley wanted to see some of his North Carolina kin, and there is circumstantial evidence that the Linebacks and Crafts held a Saturday or Sunday dinner at the Ellis and Della Lineback house, as was tradition to celebrate any family event of significance. Upon Charley's return from North Carolina, he apparently told the family some of what had gone on.

Harold (1995) remembered some very significant facts:

> *My dad went back and was recognized by several of the people, by several of the family back there. I know he really enjoyed his trip. . . . Seems as though he had one spot in one eye or something. He'd been gone [from North Carolina] for a long time. None of [the family] had recognized him or something and one of my aunts or one of his halfsister turned him around where the sun would [allow her] to see in his eye and she recognized him. And she said, "Yes, that's Charley Craft." She recognized him!*

Charley would have been welcomed among all of the Linebacks and Crafts as a "lost" relative, after his lengthy absence. One family member, Sam Craft, may have had some trepidation about seeing Charley, particularly if he felt any guilt about his last minute transaction with his father for the Craft 15-acre tract. If he had any knowledge that the tract was supposed to be Charley's inheritance, he apparently never told anyone. Harold's wife Velma (2002) wondered about Charley's inheritance:

> *Do you think Sam paid Charley for the land that might have been his inheritance? It seems to me that Charley went back to North Carolina and he got some money on that trip. I think. What makes me think that . . . I heard the girls [Buelah and Maurie] say that—that he got some money.*

One of Charley's favorite aunts, Senia Craft Whitman, died on 14 March 1922. It is not likely that Charley and Dr. Dougan stayed for more than a month in North Carolina, but Charley would certainly have gone to see Aunt Senia while he was there in February. She was probably sick at the time and perhaps even on her deathbed. Although Senia's husband, Norman Eugene Whitman, outlived her by seven years (1930), it is remotely possible that Aunt Senia gave Charley some money or left him some sort of inheritance. Family oral history indicates that Aunt Senia had inquired about Charley's share of the Junius Craft estate before her death, providing evidence that she worried about Charley's being left out of Junius's will. Maurie also wondered what had happened to land in North Carolina that might have been passed to Charley.[104]

There is also the question of whether Charley's bound boy status might have reduced his rights as one of Junius's heirs. Being a bound boy did create some distinct separation from the birth family in the minds of people in rural North Carolina in the late 1800s. The fact that Daniel and Theresa Doub never fully adopted

Charley, as evidenced by the fact that they never changed his surname to Doub, indicates that there was no legal agreement involved. Regardless of whether this is true or not, under North Carolina law, Charley would have been a legal heir to a part of Junius's estate

There may have been another reason for Charley to travel back to North Carolina, and that would have been related to the reason for his leaving the state in the first place. We have no idea whether his wife, Martha, knew about this reason. It is apparent, however, that with the accompaniment of Dr. Dougan, one of Gate's most respected citizens, Charley felt he would avoid any social criticism for his visit. Regardless of whether this was a reason or not, it is very likely that he inquired about the people involved in his leaving North Carolina in 1890, and he may have visited with some of them. Charley made every effort to make this trip honorable and respectable, as he was concerned about what his Quaker friends might think back in Gate (as evidenced by later events there). It was a matter of honor.

Visiting North Carolina

As it turned out, Charley did inherit some land from Junius's estate. Of course, Sam Craft had purchased two parcels of Junius's land, one on 13 July 1915 containing 17 and 76/100 acres and the other containing 15 and 2/5 acres only weeks before Junius died. Both of these tracts were removed from Junius's estate before it was settled in 1922.

By February 1922, the Junius Craft estate was being settled, a complicated division among seven children,

including Charley Craft, as well as Junius and Martha
Styers Craft's six offspring: Odella Craft Lineback, Etta
Craft Leinbach, Virginia (Jenny) Craft Robertson, Daisy
Craft Endsley, Sam Craft, and Blanche Craft Livingood.
Since all of the legal paper work was dated 11 February
1922, this would have been the approximate time of and
reason for Charley's trip to North Carolina. Furthermore,
Charley had to return to Beaver County with at least
eight separate legal documents to have a notary witness
Martha's and Charley's signatures on the paper work
dividing up the Junius Craft property, including a parcel
for each of Junius's children. The papers were signed and
notarized in Beaver County, Oklahoma, on 22 February
1922. The papers were identical for each of the parcels,
except for the name of the heir and the description of the
land he/she was to receive.

Charley inherited 13 acres in the settlement
of Junius Craft's estate, as described in the recorded
deed.[105]

> *Beginning at a rock and iron stake on the north
> side of the Brookstown Road, S.I. Craft's corner.
> Running North 85 degrees and 45 minutes West,
> 5.71 chains to a stone, thence North two degrees
> and 42 minutes East 22.25 chains to a stone corner
> in Pfaff's line, thence South 87 degrees and 46
> minutes East 5.71 chains to a stone, Pfaff's corner,
> thence South one and one half degrees West 15.69
> chains to a stone, Pfaff's corner, thence North 85
> degrees West 32 links to a stone, thence South 3
> degrees West 6.72 chains to the place of beginning:
> containing 13 acres, more or less.*

This piece of property laid just to the east the old Craft home place, sandwiched between the inherited property by Della Craft Lineback and Samuel Craft (See Fig. 6.4).

Charley and Martha had no use for the land in North Carolina, as it was clear that they never intended to live there. They had already sold the tract of land that Charley had bought from Boyd and Theresa Doub. Charley and Martha made the deal to sell the Doub 12 in 1902 to Junius and Martha Styers Craft, the same land for which Charley had paid $40.00 in January 1890. Junius and Martha then sold the same property in 1907 to William Parks for $182.00, clearly in an unselfish effort to help Charley.

Since Charley and Martha owned the new tract of 13 acres received from Junius Craft's estate, they saw it as a potential source of cash. Two years later on 1 April 1924, Charley and Martha signed the legal paper work in Beaver County, Oklahoma, selling the inherited property to "Samuel I Craft and his wife Kathleen E. Craft . . . for one dollar and other valuable considerations. . . ." Again, this was a typical method used to avoid taxes on the transfer of such property. We have no idea what Sam Craft really paid for Charley's property, but apparently Charley had seen the property when he visited and would have had an idea of the fair price. The best guess is that Charley would have received $1,000 to $2,000 from Sam Craft for the property.

Why didn't the rest of the family know about this transaction? There was considerable lack of trust for Sam Craft by the other family members. In other words, the transaction between Sam and his father and mother only weeks before Junius's death had colored Sam's reputation. Most of the family felt that Sam had taken advantage of his father on his deathbed when he bought the property surrounding the Craft home place. Because the deed used the phrase "one dollar and other considerations," no one knew the amount Sam paid for the property, leading relatives to believe that Sam may have received it free of charge or for a pittance. Regardless, by buying some of Junius's land, family members believed that Sam had reduced the value of Junius's total estate and had received some preferential treatment in the process. Whether this evaluation was fair to Sam or not, we simply do not know. It is possible that he paid fair market value for all of the property he bought from his father and mother, as well as from Charley and Martha. Because the legal paper work was signed by Charley and Martha in Jefferson County, Colorado, however, the North Carolina relatives were left in the dark about the transaction.

As a footnote, several family members tried to purchase the tract of land south of Brookstown Road lying between James Pfaff's and Ellis Lineback's tracts from Sam Craft, but he later sold it for $100.00 to his own son, Samuel I. ("Buck") Craft, Jr., on 8 September 1956. Buck, in turn, sold the property to Lawrence (Larry) Hand, whose family currently resides on the property.

As his share of the estate, Sam received the old Craft home place and 13 acres of land on the north side of Brookstown Road, clearly the choice portion of the Craft property. He built a new house adjacent to the old Craft house in the 1950s.

Although there perhaps was some doubt in Charley's mind about the circumstances surrounding the birth of Junius George, his alleged illegitimate son, he would have had some interest in what had happened to the boy during his visit to North Carolina.

As described by the Hicks family in 2002, Salina, Junius George's grandmother, claimed him as her child from time to time. Perhaps this was simply a ruse used by Salina to help clear her daughter Ellen's reputation and make her more eligible for marriage.[106] Ellen, Junius George's mother, married Lewis W. Cline on 14 August 1898, eleven years after Junius George's birth. It is unlikely that Junius George ever lived with the Cline family thereafter, but he stayed in the Salina George home, being cared for by Ellen's sister Cora until he was 17 years old or so.

When Charley came back to North Carolina with Dr. Dougan in 1922, in all likelihood he would have made some inquiries into the whereabouts of Junius George. Although he may have still questioned whether he was really Junius George's father, we know Charley to have been an honorable man. He had carried this secret of Junius George's birth for 35 years. If Charley met or saw Junius George on this trip, the two men's physical resemblance probably would have shocked both of them. Whether or not Charley attempted to see Junius George, he certainly would have left no record of it, as his Oklahoma family was unaware of any North Carolina descendent of Charley. We will never know whether Charley saw Junius George on his trip, but Junius George and his young family were living less than five miles from the Junius Craft place when Charley visited.

Junius Levita George married Lelia Barr on 18 December 1909 in Forsyth County. In 1920, the family

was living in Vienna Township (Pfafftown) and two of
Lelia's nephews, Marion T. and John P. Barr, were living
with them.[107]

On 25 January 1924, Junius George and Lelia had
a daughter named Anne Ellen George **(Fig. 6.5)**. Anne
Ellen's case is very interesting, but disappointing. The
Hicks family described her as having a "wild reputation"
and "running with a bad group." She worked at Union
Carbide in Winston-Salem for a short while around 1942,
then at Hanes Hosiery, and finally at R.J. Reynolds Tobacco
Company until 1946. Without warning, she suddenly
disappeared. Her family was very concerned about
her, filed a missing persons report, and even requested
help from the North Carolina Bureau of Investigation.
The search grew cold, and Anne Ellen seemed to have
disappeared from the face of the earth.[108]

In 2005, however, Anne Ellen's distant relatives
Theresa Hutchins, Jerry Loafman, and this author were
able to trace Anne Ellen through the Social Security
Death Index to Seattle, Washington, where she had died
in 1983 at 59 years of age.[109] Anne Ellen had no known
children, according to the family of Barbara Morrison,
who had been Anne Ellen and George Moose's foster
child, close friend, and confidant. Why Anne Ellen left
North Carolina and never communicated again with her
relatives remains a mystery.

At 76 years of age, Junius George died of
coronary occlusion due to arteriosclerosis heart disease
on 29 July 1964.[110] His alleged father, Charley Craft, died
14 years younger of similar heart disease. At the time of

Junius George's death, his address was listed at Route 1, Pfafftown, within the same community where Charley had been raised.

Fig. 6.5. Anne Ellen George at approximately eight years of age. *(Permission by Jerry Loafman)*

As a final footnote to this part of Charley's story, without comment in May 2002, this author showed a picture of Anne Ellen George to Jeanne Baker, Charley and Martha's granddaughter. Jeanne thought the picture of Anne Ellen was a picture of herself (Jeanne) as a child. We were astounded at the close resemblance, providing further circumstantial evidence of a genetic connection between Anne Ellen and Jeanne **(Fig. 6.6, 6.7, 6.8, 6.9, and 6.10).**

Fig. 6.6. Lelia, Junius, and Anne Ellen George. *(Permission of Jerry Loafman).*

Fig. 6.7. Junius George, Anne Ellen George, and Lelia George about 1945. *(Permission of Jerry Loafman)*

Fig. 6.8. Jeanne Baker as a young woman of 17 years of age.
(Permission by Jeanne Baker)

Fig. 6.9. Jeanne Baker in a newspaper clipping announcing her recent promotion at a bank in Glenwood Springs, 12 January 1967. *(Permission by Jeanne Baker)*

Fig. 6.10. George Moose and Charley Craft's granddaughter Anne Ellen George. This photo was taken prior to their marriage sometime between 1946 and 1950. According to the author's research, based mostly on family oral history, Anne Ellen left home on a Sunday in 1946 or 1947 and was never heard from again by her North Carolina relatives. Apparently, she married George Moose and they lived in Phoenix, Arizona and Seattle, Washington, as documented by photos and postcards. She and George never had children, but they did take in a foster child, Barbara Morrison. George died on May 25, 1972 and Anne Ellen died in a nursing home in Seattle in 1983. *(Permission of Barbara Morrison).*

Family Troubles in Gate

By 1923, it was growing clear to the Crafts that hard times were coming on the prairie. There had been two wet years back to back and mechanized agriculture was increasing the acreages farmers could plant. This was still six or seven years before the famous Dust Bowl of the Dirty Thirties appeared. One out of every three years had been a poor crop year throughout the Craft years on the homestead, but there was more than just climate fluctuations involved in farming. Price fluctuations for crops also played a role in the successful and unsuccessful years on Panhandle farms. When large regional wheat harvests were successful, prices often plummeted. Two good years in a row usually meant dry years were around the corner, and the Crafts had to know it.

Charley continued to look for a way to collect his "grubstake" from the farm and move on to greener pastures. His first attempt to sell it had failed, but he had not given up hope.

Charley and Martha's oldest son, Paul, had served in the military and attended college at the Oklahoma A&M in Stillwater. He was 27 years old, living in Stillwater, Oklahoma, and worldly compared to the rest of the Craft children. He was to play a major role in Charley's decision to sell the farm again.

Buelah, who was 19 years old, had graduated from the Laurence Friends Academy and was teaching school part-time at the Berends School north of the Craft farm. She was a pretty teenager with a strong will much like her mother. She may have felt somewhat trapped on the Craft farm in tiny Gate, where social opportunities were relatively limited. Nonetheless, a local boy, Leslie Carpenter, 22 years old, became a suitor.

The families of Cornelius Carpenter and his brother Robert C. (Case) Carpenter attended the Baptist Church in Rosston, Oklahoma, about eight miles east of Gate. The Cornelius Carpenter family lived about five miles east of the Crafts. There were eight children in the Carpenter family, including son Leslie, plus the families of aunts and uncles scattered around the community.

Leslie was 5 feet, 10 inches tall, handsome, bright, and energetic. He clearly had a good and outgoing personality and was an attractive marriage prospect for local girls. Although he was not a Quaker, Leslie had attended the Laurence Academy with Buelah in 1920-21, and he had worked away from home at least one summer.

In 1920 at the age of 19, Leslie worked in Payne County, Oklahoma, possibly at an oil field, boarding with a local family.[111] Consequently, he had field experience away from home before he was 20 years old, had some money and perhaps a car, and was more worldly than most of the boys around Gate. He spent a great deal of time around Gate, although it was nearly 10 miles by road from the Carpenter home, according to his brother Randall, and the local boys were jealous of the attention paid to him by the local girls.[112] At least once if not several times, Leslie had altercations with the local boys. There was little love lost between Leslie and Paul Craft, who believed Leslie was "wild."[113]

In June or July of 1923, Buelah learned that she was pregnant. She probably could not have told Leslie, as in all likelihood he had already left Gate and was traveling on the wheat circuit. As job opportunities in Gate were lacking, Leslie had planned all spring to join the 1923 wheat harvest in order to accumulate enough money to bankroll his own farm. He probably left in early June, just before Buelah learned of her pregnancy.

The type of work associated with grain harvest on the wheat circuit was similar to what Charley had experienced back in 1889, when he went to Indiana to help in the wheat and corn harvest. Leslie had had some experience of working away from home. There is no doubt that Charley and Martha saw the wheat harvest as a good way for Leslie to get a grubstake. They also may have been happy to see him depart Gate for a while to cool down his relationship with Buelah.

The annual wheat harvest generally began in early June in central Texas and gradually moved north through Oklahoma, Kansas, Nebraska, the Dakotas, and adjacent states, and into Saskatchewan, Canada. By late October and early November, the threshing crews and their machinery ended up in central Canada. Putting in 18-hour days seven days a week for four months typically left these 10- to 15-man crews exhausted, but the money was extremely good. A good hand who was reasonably frugal with his money on the wheat harvest circuit could return home with $500 to $1,000 in his pocket. While on the road, the crew's whereabouts were often unknown to the families back home, as they were constantly on the move. By the time a postcard from a worker arrived home, the crew could be hundreds of miles away. Consequently, the men seldom received mail from home and essentially remained incognito throughout the four-month road trip.

There were distractions along the way, as well, including whiskey and gambling. Some members of the crews were old-timers who knew the bars and hotels in the bigger towns, and they no doubt introduced the new, inexperienced hands to some of the distractions. It is perfectly likely that Leslie had no knowledge of Buelah's pregnancy throughout the summer of 1923.

It was clear to the Craft and Carpenter families that Buelah and Leslie were deeply in love, so both families were worried that something could happen. In fact, in the summer of 1923, Buelah was in such a state of mental anguish that the Crafts sent her to visit the Ellis and Della Lineback family in North Carolina. Charley and Martha probably didn't know that Buelah was pregnant at this time. Buelah went by train and visited the several Lineback children, but she was particularly drawn to Mayola Katherine Lineback, Ellis and Della's fifth child, who was born 16 December 1903. Buelah and Mayola were almost exactly the same ages, and they bonded instantly.[114] In fact, Mayola also became pregnant that fall before marrying Orrin Edward Doub. Buelah probably confided to Mayola that she was pregnant, given that she would have been beside herself with anxiety and needed a friend she could trust. Buelah and Mayola remained close the remainder of their lives.[115]

Certainly, by the time Buelah returned to Gate in late summer, she was at least three months pregnant and knew she had to tell her parents. Soon, the Carpenters knew. Edith Carpenter thought a great deal of Buelah, who often had visited to help her with her canning.[116] The news of Buelah's pregnancy surely pained Mrs. Carpenter, for she probably felt some responsibility, as she had encouraged Buelah's relationship with Leslie. She had believed that Buelah was just the sort of girl Leslie needed to settle down. Edith liked Buelah, and, under the circumstances of the pregnancy, she was clearly ready to welcome Buelah into her family. The problem was that Leslie was unreachable on the wheat circuit.

Leslie returned to his family home in Gate in mid-October 1923. It is unclear whether he went to see Buelah during his first few days back. In fact, it is questionable whether he even knew she was pregnant until he saw her. In all likelihood, however, his mother told him immediately and plans had already been developed to take the couple outside the county to be married, if they were both willing—and they were. Under the conditions of a rushed marriage because of an unexpected pregnancy, the brief civil ceremony was normally carried out some distance away from the bride and groom's community, as there was social stigma attached to pre-marriage pregnancies. Pre-marriage pregnancies were not uncommon in Quaker communities where social order was the norm, but there probably was a greater level of stigma attached to such events than in non-Quaker communities. There was something else, however, on Leslie's mind.

Martha Craft and Edith Carpenter took Leslie and Buelah to be married out of Beaver County, Oklahoma. According to Maurie Craft Lang, the family believed that the couple was married in Woodward, Oklahoma.[117] Randall Carpenter (2002), Leslie's brother, remembered that the couple eloped to Minneola, Kansas, 44 miles north of Gate. This confusion indicates the level of secrecy involved in the ceremony. Buelah and Leslie were actually married in a civil ceremony on 20 October 1923 in Meade, Kansas, about 40 miles northwest of Gate, according to the marriage certificate (**Fig. 6.11, 6.12, and 6.13**).

Leslie had contracted a disease on the wheat circuit. Dr. Dougan was the Carpenter family doctor, but Leslie chose not to be examined by him because Dr. Dougan was also a close friend of the Craft family. Instead, he went to see 43-year-old Dr. George A. Nylund, a former Army physician, who had been practicing in Gate a relatively short time.[118] Dr. Nylund's father was from Illinois and his mother was from Sweden. He would have been well accepted among the homesteaders around Gate, many with Midwest and Scandinavian heritages themselves. At least in the 1920 U.S. Census, Dr. Nylund was listed as boarding in Gate and not being married.[119] Presumably by 1923, he had gained some stability, as well as reputation. Having more than one doctor in the community offered an additional option to patients.

Upon examining Leslie, Dr. Nylund had extremely alarming news. His diagnosis was syphilis! In 1923, having syphilis was a death sentence, as there was no penicillin at the time. The disease was particularly contagious through sexual intercourse. Syphilis would cause skin lesions initially, but over time it could cause degenerative changes in the central nervous system and other body organs, finally resulting in a painful death.

Leslie's diagnosis absolutely would have devastated him, his family, Buelah, and the Crafts. At a moment in time when things had begun looking up for the young couple, this diagnosis threw an appalling chill over all of Gate. In all likelihood, Dr. Nylund informed Dr. Dougan, who went directly to see Charley Craft.

Marriage Affidavit and License Record.

18441 Crane & Company Topeka

MARRIAGE AFFIDAVIT

The State of Kansas, Meade County, ss.

IN THE PROBATE COURT OF SAID COUNTY AND STATE.

L. A. Carpenter hereby applies for a MARRIAGE LICENSE

addressed to any minister or magistrate authorized by law to unite in matrimony

L. A. Carpenter and _Beulah Craft_

and being duly sworn deposes:

That said _L. A. Carpenter_ is 21 years of age, and that said _Beulah Craft_ is aged 17 years; that they have their parents' consent to said union, and that neither has been divorced within six months last past.

That said contracting parties are not related to each other in any of the degrees prohibited by law, namely: parent and child, grandparent and grandchild in any degree, brother and sister of the whole or half blood, uncle or niece, aunt or nephew, nor first cousins.

That neither of said parties is or ever has been epileptic, imbecile, feeble-minded, or insane; or, if either is or has ever been so afflicted, then that the woman is more than forty-five years of age.

And that neither party was born subsequent to the insanity of either of his or her parents; or, if so, that the woman about to be married is more than forty-five years of age.

L. A. Carpenter

Subscribed and sworn to before me, this 20" day of Oct. 19 23

[SEAL.]

Filed Oct. 20 ", 19 23

No. _J. C. Frith_ Probate Judge.

R. No. 7487

P. J. No. 257

State of Kansas, Central Division of Vital Statistics

MARRIAGE LICENSE

In the Probate Court of Meade County. Meade, Kansas, Oct. 20", 19 23

To Any Person Authorized by Law to Perform the Marriage Ceremony, Greeting:

YOU ARE HEREBY AUTHORIZED TO JOIN IN MARRIAGE

L. A. Carpenter of Rosston, Okla., Age 21

Beulah Craft of Gate, " Age 17

with the consent of

and of this license, duly indorsed, you will make return to my office at Meade, Kansas, within ten days after performing the ceremony.

[SEAL.]

Probate Judge.

INDORSEMENT.

TO WHOM IT MAY CONCERN:

I hereby certify that I performed the ceremony joining in marriage the above-named couple, on the 20" day of Oct. 1923, at Meade, Kans.

Fig. 6.11. Buelah and Leslie's marriage certificate. *(Source: Central Division of Vital Statistics, State of Oklahoma)*

165

Fig. 6.12. Buelah Craft standing beside the family's Ford touring car on the Craft farm, probably on her wedding day. *(Permission by Jeanne Baker)*

Figure 6.13. Leslie Carpenter, a handsome young man, probably taken on his and Buelah Craft's wedding day. *(Permission by Jeanne Baker.)*

Harold Craft and Maurie Craft Lang (1985) remembered well the somber entry of Dr. Dougan into the Craft house. Charley sent the children outside and the adults talked.

Charley in later years told Harold that Dr. Dougan told them the news and gave them serious advice, according to Harold (1996):

> *You can't let Buelah see Leslie, as she could catch it [syphilis].*

There is no evidence that Dr. Dougan had made his own diagnosis, but had apparently relied upon Dr. Nylund's. In all probability, Dr. Dougan had seen syphilis on some of the Indian lands where he had worked, but syphilis would have been relatively rare in Gate and probably entirely absent in the Quaker community. Having been an Army physician, Dr. Nylund should have had experience in diagnosing the disease. The seriousness of a syphilis diagnosis cannot be overstated here, although it was sometimes misdiagnosed. It has been called the "Great Imitator," as its clinical manifestations are legion, causing it to simulate those of many other diseases. Regardless of who made the diagnosis, the damage was done.

Over the next six months—from November through April—Charley, Martha, and the Carpenters kept Buelah and Leslie apart. This was an excruciating time for the families, but it must have been beyond hope for Buelah and Leslie.

Three years later in the fall of 1926, Dr. Nylund also diagnosed another local man, Edward F. Hanzl, with syphilis. The Hanzl family was Swedish-American, neighbors and friends of the Carpenters. They lived about three miles east in Harper County, and when he returned from the Army with a strange ailment, Ed Hanzl went to see Dr. Nylund. Ed was 32 years old and certainly would have trusted the Swedish-American doctor. His mother, Mary Hanzl, was a widow in 1926, and Dr. Nylund was their family doctor. By this time, Leslie Carpenter's medical diagnosis would have been common knowledge throughout both Harper and Beaver counties. Ed was the only son in the Hanzl family, and the diagnosis of his syphilis would have been devastating news to that family as well. Ed left his mother's house, went into isolation in the barn, and took his meals from the porch for a few weeks. On October 30, Ed Hanzl shot and killed himself.[120] His suicide demonstrated the level of agony that accompanied the diagnosis of syphilis in the 1920s.

Charley and Martha didn't know what to do in the month or so after learning about Leslie's diagnosis. Meanwhile, everyone in the small Gate community soon knew about the rushed marriage between Buelah and Leslie and about Leslie's deadly diagnosis. There was certainly social stigma involved in these events in the Quaker community. How severe the actual social prejudice, it is hard to know. The Quakers were very forgiving, according to Wayne Lewis (2002). Social pressure, however, can be actual or perceived; in either regard, it can be intense— particularly when the welfare of the Quaker community is threatened. With Charley's personal history of enduring social stigma in North Carolina as a bound boy, as an adult he probably perceived the pressure in Gate's Quaker community as unbearable.

Upon learning of Leslie's diagnosis, one of the first things Charley and Martha did was to contact their oldest son, Paul. Paul was the family's most educated and worldly child, having served in the military and attending college at Oklahoma Agriculture and Technology University (now Oklahoma State University). He was a kind and family-oriented individual, who later reveled in his nieces' and nephews' successes, although he never had children of his own. Throughout his life, he was very concerned about his brothers and sisters and their children. However, he was known, on occasion, to embellish their successes in life. Paul was also very opinionated. Once he made up his mind, it was difficult to dissuade him.

When Paul learned of the family's dilemma—probably by mail since a telegraph would have been too public—he flew into a rage. It is likely that he rushed to Gate, as he was living in Stillwater at the time. No doubt, his advice to the family was to take Buelah and her baby out of Gate as soon as possible after the baby's approaching birth. Having been in the military, Paul knew syphilis was a highly contagious and deadly sexual disease, and he would have presented powerful arguments to the less-worldly Charley and Martha. The advice to keep Buelah and Leslie apart was certainly logical, given what little Gate residents knew about the disease at that time, most of which was learned by word of mouth.

Given the extreme social circumstances swirling around their family and with a baby coming, Charley and Martha began to plan how to separate Buelah and Leslie permanently. In their minds, as well as in Paul's, they were all "saving Buelah's and the baby's lives."

The most logical temporary solution was to move Buelah and the baby to Denver, where Martha's sister, Emma (Aunt Em) Frost lived. Emma and her two children, Arl and Zola (Frostie), had been very close to the Craft family, constantly writing postcards to the family and visiting them both in Gate and Palacios, Texas. Emma had moved to Denver and had been urging the Crafts to move there even before 1923.[121]

It may have initially crossed Charley and Martha's minds that they could send Buelah and the baby to Denver to stay with Emma. At some point, that solution apparently was expanded to selling the Craft farm and moving the entire family to Denver. The decision may have crystallized with the birth of Buelah and Leslie's baby, Vera Jeanne Carpenter, on 19 February 1924. Buelah gave birth at the Craft family home, attended by Dr. Dougan and possibly Dr. Dougan's wife.[122]

Jeanne became Charley and Martha's special granddaughter, a relationship that continued throughout the couple's lives. Not only was Jeanne born in their house, but the Crafts no doubt felt a strong responsibility for her welfare. Jeanne and Buelah lived with the Crafts through the first years of Jeanne's life after the move to Denver (Arvada).

As a footnote to the Crafts' decision to leave Gate, Maurie Craft Lang blamed Paul for rushing the Crafts into moving to Denver.[123] Randall Carpenter (2002), Leslie's younger brother, blamed Charley Craft for spreading the word about Leslie's illness and the severity of it. He believed that Charley's dissemination of information about the deadliness of the disease even had something to do with Ed Hanzl's suicide three years after the Crafts departed Gate. Nevertheless, Charley most certainly would not have known the etiology of syphilis, and anything he had to say about it had to derive from someone else. Was it Dr. Dougan's initial warning that Charley repeated? Did Paul's very vocal and persistent warnings about the danger of the disease influence Charley to warn others about it? On the other hand, given Leslie's charisma and playboy reputation and the Quakers' social mores, was there a general hysteria that flooded the community upon learning about Leslie's diagnosis?

What about Leslie? How might he have felt during this whirlwind of recriminations and decisions that were out of his control? In all likelihood, he would have been extremely frightened by what Dr. Nylund had told him. Leslie certainly would not have wanted Buelah and the unborn baby to contract the disease from him. There is no indication that he was dishonorable under the circumstances. He had supposedly contracted the disease without even knowing about Buelah's pregnancy. Years later, Jeanne wondered why Leslie didn't fight harder to stay with Buelah.[124] If Leslie were an honorable young man, he would have voluntarily separated from Buelah out of fear about the contagiousness and "death sentence" of syphilis.

The complete answers to these questions remain unknown, but this is not the end of Buelah and Leslie's story.

CHAPTER 7

GIVING UP AND LEAVING OKLAHOMA FOR GOOD

Making Plans to Move to Denver

Details surrounding the Crafts' plans to sell the farm and move to Denver are limited. This was certainly a turning point for Charley and Martha, where it seems that both gave up on the farm and seemingly wanted out at all costs. Their final year on the farm had been traumatic beyond comparison. After all of the previous events in their lives, none compared with the overwhelming anxiety that was thrust upon this family-oriented couple in 1923 and early 1924.

The first three months of 1924 must have been extremely hectic on the farm, as Charley and Martha decided how to accomplish the complicated process of moving a month-old baby and her mother to Denver in an open touring car in the early spring. Furthermore, arrangements had to be made to sell the Craft farm animals and equipment and the farm itself, which was complicated by unpaid mortgages.

At some point, Charley and Martha decided that Charley would take Buelah, newborn Jeanne and 12-

year-old Harold on the 400-mile road trip from Gate to Denver. Under the best weather conditions, the trip would have taken at least two long days by car. Because the trip was to be in April, however, unpaved roads through the Oklahoma Panhandle and southeastern Colorado, changeable spring weather conditions, and a baby in an open touring car made the trip extremely treacherous. But it demonstrates the urgency by Charley and Martha to spirit Buelah and baby Jeanne away from Gate.

Martha was to stay behind with Maurie, Cecil, and Forrest and arrange to sell the farm animals and equipment and many of the household furnishings as quickly as possible. She, Cecil, and Forrest would then travel to Englewood, Kansas, and catch a train for Denver. Maurie stayed on to finish her final year at the Laurence Friends Academy.

The Move to Denver

The move from Gate to Denver was welcomed by most of the Craft children. Buelah, of course, would have had very mixed feelings. Certainly, she would have been devastated that so many things had happened to her and her family within such a short period, and she may have felt guilt about her involvement. There is no question, however, that she would have been furious at Leslie for his apparent betrayal and infidelity while he was on the wheat circuit, although he may have known nothing about her pregnancy during the time. Leslie's contraction of syphilis made reconciliation impossible for Buelah. Her situation must have been terribly depressing for a young woman caught up in things she couldn't understand.

On the other hand, the younger Craft children, welcomed the move to Denver, as told by Harold (1995):

I can only speak for myself. And I was tickled to death to get out [of Gate]. Of course, my mother's sister lived out here in Arvada, which is a suburb of Denver. We were in touch with them and they used to come visit with us [in Gate]. I say, them—its my aunt and her daughter who used to come visit us in Gate—and their description of the area around Denver was always nice. I found it to be, after we moved out here, just what they had described it to be. And I know it was so much nicer, but I thought we lived or moved to the Garden of Eden when we moved out here after living so much out there on the prairie.

We are less certain about Charley and Martha's frames of mind. Both had worked hard to make the farm in Gate a prosperous enterprise, despite the vagaries of weather and climate. It appears that they were very disappointed with the Gate community, in general, and the Quaker community, in particular, regarding attitudes toward the Crafts after Buelah's pregnancy. As evidence, both Martha and Charley abandoned the Quaker Church after they moved to Denver. Certainly, both wanted to get their grubstake out of the farm. But more than anything else, they were a family-oriented couple and they realized that distance from Gate could provide relief from many of the family's problems, which also might help Buelah to mend.

The family began moving to the Denver area in April 1924, and times had grown difficult on the farm in Gate. Charley had been worried by the cyclic nature of the climate in Beaver County, Oklahoma, as were all the farmers around Gate. Should they plant less or more? The ceaseless wind during the bad years not only uncovered the wheat seeds in the fields, but the blowing soil cut the tender shoots off at ground level after seeds sprouted. Three or more good crop years in a row were unheard of, so most farmers were bracing for some dry ones by the spring of 1924.

When asked about the reasons for the Crafts leaving the farm, Harold (1995) was somewhat evasive:

> *Well, you just wasn't able to raise a crop [some years]. And I don't know just all together. My aunt had been wanting us to come to Colorado for some time, as I remember. My mother and my aunt corresponded all the time and they kept asking us to come out. And, finally, I guess, my mother and father just decided that it would be a pretty good move. When Jeanne was born in 1924, Buelah, Jeanne, my Dad, and I come out here [to Denver] then. Drove out ahead. My mother and the rest of the family stayed down there and held the farm sale and sold whatever else. Equipment and everything at the farm. Then they caught the train and come out later. We come out in April of 1924. My mother [and the rest of the family] come out later that summer.*

The trip to the Denver area in the open 1917 Ford touring car was difficult and memorable to Harold (**Fig. 7.1**). Harold (1995) described the trip as a near disaster:

> *No top [on the touring car]! We got caught in a snowstorm and had to stay in Colorado Springs.*

My dad sent Jeanne and Buelah [on to Denver].
You see, Jeanne was born in February of 1924.
He called my aunt [from Colorado Springs]. See,
Jeanne would have been—we come in April and
Jeanne was just a tiny baby from February to
April. [We got caught in a snowstorm] in that open
car. When the storm hit us in Colorado Springs,
my dad put Jeanne and Buelah on the train and
called my aunt in Denver. They went down and
got [them] at the depot in Denver. So my dad and
I spent two or three days and nights in Colorado
Springs. Then we got up and come on up in the
open car. Come on to Denver after the storm had
subsided and was over. [The car] was packed
pretty heavy, as I remember.

Charley, Harold, Buelah, and baby Jeanne settled
in with Emma, as Charley began the process of finding
work and a place for the family to rent in Arvada.

Auctioning the Craft Farm's Equipment and Animals

Martha remained in Gate and held an auction to
sell the farm equipment and animals and some of the
household goods. Farm equipment would have included
a turning plow, lister, harrows, and hand implements. The
cream separator, bottles, canning jars, and crocks also
would have been sold, and Martha may have sold their
portion of the threshing machine to the other partners.
Cattle and horses would have sold, although the prices
would have been low, as spring cattle would have just been
through the winter and would have been lean. Martha did
not sell the farmland and buildings at this time.[125]

Fig. 7.1. Harold Craft beside a 1917 Ford touring car in the Gate Museum in Gate, Oklahoma, 1990. This car is identical to the one that Charley Craft drove to take Harold, Buelah, and her baby Jeanne from Gate to Denver in the spring of 1924. They were caught in a snowstorm in the open car and marooned in Colorado Springs. *(Source: Permission by Velma Craft)*

Most of the neighbors in general and the Quaker families specifically would have attended the auction. Probably many came before the sale to help Martha get ready. This would have been a troublesome day for all of the Quakers, as they witnessed the loss of one of their most respected families under very difficult circumstances. Martha had to handle this job with only the help of Maurie and Cecil, as Forrest was too young to be much help. No doubt, most of the community felt sorry for her and were willing to help however they could. Yet, this one act of holding the auction best illustrates Martha's inner strength and willingness to take on a difficult task. She literally took charge of the preparations for the sale.

Martha probably had a local auctioneer handle the sale, as was the custom. It is possible that A.B. Card arranged the presence of an auctioneer or even served in that capacity himself. After all, Charley and Martha had treated him most compassionately when he and the Pratts defaulted on the purchase of the Craft farm back in 1913.

It is not clear when the auction was held, but it was probably in early May. Harold believed that Martha held the sale and she, Cecil, and Forrest followed Charley on to Denver by rail. This part of the move would have been a trying episode for Martha, although Maurie and Cecil would have been available to help pack up the family belongings. Many of these would have been the family's personal items that Charley had been unable to pack into the Ford during his initial trip to Denver a month or so earlier.

Mortgaging the Farm

With the farm equipment and animals gone, the next object was to sell the farm. The unsuccessful episode with the Pratts left the Crafts with little confidence that they could successfully sell their farm to a private individual. Under most purchases by individual buyers, the seller(s) would be expected to hold a note on the property. As the Pratt purchase indicated, however, such propositions were risky for both buyer and seller. Moreover, it was clear this time the Crafts would not be able to return to Gate, should a buyer default on the purchase.

A deed record from the Beaver County Records Office indicates that Charley and Martha did not return to Gate in the summer of 1923 to clear up their finances.

179

Apparently, the transfer of the Craft farm was carried out long-distance, probably handled once more by A.B. Card in Oklahoma. The deed record (a mortgage) was made on 16 June, signed and notarized on 30 June in Jefferson County, Colorado, and recorded in the Records Office in Beaver County, Oklahoma, on 9 July 1924. The State Bank of Commerce, Gate, held the mortgage for $3,000:[126]

> *This Indenture, made this 16th day of June A.D. 1924 between Charles V. Craft and Martha Craft, husband and wife of Beaver County, in the State of Oklahoma, of the first part, and State Bank of Commerce, Gate, Oklahoma, party of the second part: Witnessseth, that said party of the first part, in consideration of the sum of Three Thousand & no/100 dollars, the receipt whereof is hereby acknowledged do by these presents grant, bargain, sell and convey unto the said party of the second part heirs and assigns all the following described Real Estate, situated in the County of Beaver, State of Oklahoma, to-wit: [followed by a description of the Craft 120 acre parcel, with a note regarding a $1.50 owed to the "I.R.S."]. The grantors [Crafts] also acknowledged another mortgage on the farm for which they were responsible: Except a mortgage to the Federal Land Bank, Wichita, Kansas, of $1600.00 and accrued interest and taxes for 1923 and prior years if unpaid. [Charles V. Craft and Martha Craft's signatures are attached. Then Fred B. Robinson notarized the papers on 30 June 1924 in Jefferson County.]*

It is unclear how the mortgage deal with State Bank of Commerce, Gate, was consummated on 16 June. It is possible that Martha made the deal in Charley's absence; it is even remotely possible that Charley went back to Gate for a few days in order to mortgage the farm and help Martha and Forrest move to Denver. Indications are that someone else handled the deal in Charley and Martha's absence.

The Crafts mortgaged their farm to State Bank of Commerce, Gate, with the intention of walking away from the homestead and turning it over to the bank. This was common practice, according to Wayne Lewis (2002), but frowned upon locally for two reasons. First, banks used locally deposited money to make these loans. When the economy crashed, as it did in 1929, investors lost because the value of land declined. Secondly, Oklahoma's Bill Murray law forbade banks from holding the land for more than five years, perhaps forcing bank officials to sell land, whose mortgages had been defaulted upon, at low prices.

Therefore, the Crafts left Gate, Oklahoma, with their finances in considerable disarray after 19 years of dealing with the homestead. Although they received $3,000 on the mortgage from the bank, they still owed $1,000.00 to Pittsburg Mortgage Company in Kansas, $1,000 to the State Bank of Commerce, Gate, on another loan, and $1,600 to the Federal Land Bank.

Overall, the family walked away from their hard-won homestead without a grubstake and still owing $600.00 more than they received. This was, indeed, a disheartening time for the Crafts. As honorable people, they had to be disappointed that they would have to default on their $3,000 loan to the State Bank of Commerce, Gate.

In later years, when Harold and Maurie returned to Gate for a class reunion, one of the long time Gate residents made the statement to Maurie that "Charley shouldn't have left owing all of that money."[127] It was clear that the statement upset Maurie, but its context is made clearer now that we are able to analyze Charley's financial papers in the Beaver County Records Office. It is also clear that defaulting on mortgages to banks was a common practice of the time and all parties knew, understood, and accepted the situation.

No one in Beaver County would have anticipated that the 1929 Wall Street collapse, the Great Depression, and the Dust Bowl were just around the corner. Banks failed throughout the region during this dark period in the U.S. Great Plains' history. Many local investors lost money in local banks and later felt anger toward those farmers who got out before the collapse and who defaulted on their mortgages leaving the banks to hold the bag, so to speak. Nonetheless, banks had accepted mortgage defaulting as the norm. Had the economic collapse not occurred, banks stood to gain financially on the defaults by reselling the properties each time at a profit.

The economic collapse ended this profitable property turnover. Bank managers had perpetuated the process by "buying" the property through defaulted mortgages at fire sale prices. Complaints followed only when the banks lost money. *Caveat emptor* (let the buyer beware).

After arriving in the spring of 1924 in Arvada, northwest of Denver, Charley immediately enlisted a nearby judge to help Buelah gain a divorce from Leslie Carpenter. Buelah—so much like her mother, Martha—

was a strong and beautiful young woman, and Charley and Martha wanted to help her move on in life **(Fig. 7.2).** She taught school in the Denver area for a while, and Jeanne stayed with Charley and Martha, her grandparents. Charley, Martha, and Jeanne grew extremely close during this time.

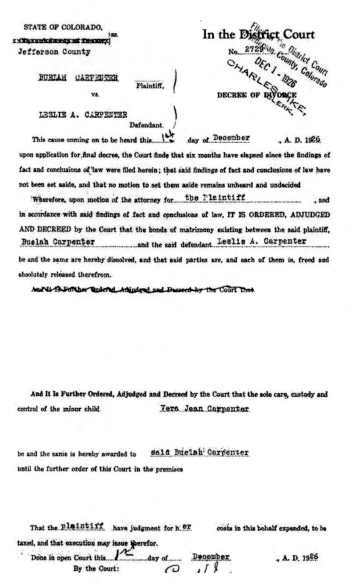

Fig. 7.2. The divorce decree was granted in Jefferson County, Colorado, between Leslie A. Carpenter, defendant, and Buelah Carpenter, plaintiff, on 23 March 1926 *(Colorado State Archives, Case No. 2729, Register of Actions: Book 6, page 178. Judgment Book B., page 175, Court Record: Book M-429.)*

CHAPTER 8

THE END OF THE JOURNEY

Life and Death in Denver, 1924-34

Charley, Harold, Buelah, and Jeanne lived briefly with Martha's sister, Emma, in Denver. Charley began searching for a house and a small acreage to rent, finding what he wanted in Arvada, a small agricultural town a few miles west of Denver. The owner was a local judge who befriended Charley and his family. Charley and Martha rented the house and property for the next nine years. Martha, Cecil, and Forrest joined the family in the late spring of 1924, after holding the auction of the farm equipment and animals in Gate. Maurie soon joined the family after completing her high school education at Laurence Friends Academy.

The family was nearly broke when Charley arrived in Colorado. In all likelihood, Charley had little, if any, disposable income when he first arrived and very little prospect for making any money that year. The 1924 crop season on the farm in Gate had been a disaster because Charley had planted his wheat during the previous fall but had not been able to harvest it before the family left. In fact, Charley's finances were in such poor shape that he was unable to pay his property and federal taxes. Certainly, Charley would have relied upon income from selling the farm and the farm auction in Gate to have enough money to live in Colorado. When Martha joined them in Denver a month or two later, she brought the money gleaned from the auction of the farm animals and equipment. By mid-summer, the Crafts had received the $3,000 from the mortgage of the Craft farm. The family then had some disposable income, but was still in debt. Charley and Martha had to continue to be very frugal with their cash.

After Charley rented the house and small acreage in Arvada, he repeatedly told family members over the years that he would never buy a house or any land until he could afford to pay cash for it.[128] This is an instructive comment, for it probably reflects on Charley's and his family's financial struggles in North Carolina, Indiana, and Oklahoma over the previous 50 years. The fact was that, after leaving Oklahoma, he and Martha were never able to accumulate enough money to buy land or a house. Consequently, they rented property the rest of their lives.

Charley was 51 years old when the family moved to Colorado, still in prime condition and still interested in doing the one thing he knew—farming. He bought a team of horses and began plowing the gardens of neighbors in Arvada.[129] On his own rented land in the spring of 1924, he planted garden crops and made some money trucking the vegetables into Denver. Cecil, age 15, Harold, age 12, and Forrest, age 10, helped their father in the fields.

Charley was a quick learner when it came to agriculture. His crops included corn, beans, squash, turnips, potatoes, lettuce, and celery. Most of these weren't new crops for him, as he had learned to plant them in North Carolina as a boy and had continued on the farm in Oklahoma. What was new for him, however, was the commercial aspect of marketing the vegetables. Up until this point in time, vegetable production had been largely for his family's use.

One of Charley's specialties became celery, grown and then buried in the ground for a period. This process bleached the celery and made it a highly attractive product in considerable demand. Charley even shipped some to his relatives in North Carolina, who remembered it as being a product they had never seen before, but admired.

Charley's children remembered him as quick with his math in calculating costs and values, able to come up with per unit costs, adding in labor and transportation costs, and providing a profit margin. Apparently, he was able to make a decent living there in Arvada. Gradually, he was able to retire his debts, paying off one loan made in 1922 by the State Bank of Commerce, Gate, and retired 5 September 1928. He paid off another from the Security National Bank, Oklahoma City, for $1,000 made in 1914, retiring it on 20 November 1928. By all accounts, in 1928, Charley was back on his feet financially.

The family had frequent gatherings in Arvada **(Fig. 8.1, 8.2, and 8.3)**, but granddaughter Jeanne (2002) remembered the couple as appearing tired and worn in these years following their move **(Fig. 8.4)**. It was as though all of the struggles over their lives had brought them few rewards outside of their children and grandchildren.

It was tough for them to readjust to a new life into their 50s, and they seemed to live only for their children. They helped three, Paul, Harold, and Cecil, through college, and Charley lived to see four of their six children married and the births of two of their sixteen grandchildren.

When the Great Depression hit the country in 1929, Charley apparently began to have financial problems again, as he had trouble selling his produce, making his rent payments, and paying his medical bills. His children's families supplemented Charley and Martha's income from time to time with small donations. Velma remembered Harold saying that Martha kept a calendar with pockets in the kitchen, in which she kept some surplus cash. The family members would add small amounts of cash from time to time to help, even though they could ill afford it.[130]

Howard Ensley, husband of Charley's half-sister, Daisy Craft, and his half-nephew, Hiatt Lineback, from North Carolina visited Charley and Martha in 1933. The two North Carolinians toured the Dust Bowl that ravaged the region, ironically centered on the Oklahoma Panhandle where the Craft homestead was located. Harold Craft remembered that he and Hiatt went to the local fair and enjoyed themselves. Charley was in failing health at the time, but he enjoyed seeing his North Carolina relatives. At least two other family members visited Charley from North Carolina in 1933: his halfsister Della Craft Lineback and Jenny Craft Ensley **(Figs. 8.5 and 8.6).** Other photos showed Charley sitting in a rocking chair in front of his and Martha's rented house **(Fig. 8.7).** His complexion was unusually dark.

Charley had grown increasingly ill beginning in 1932. He was apparently suffering from congestive heart failure, resulting in the retention of fluids and swelling of his extremities. The family was very worried about him and insisted that he have medical attention. As his illness progressed in early 1934, Charley's doctors told him that he had to have an operation.

Fig. 8.1. This was one of the family's earliest pictures, taken in Denver during the fall of 1924, of baby Jeanne and some family members perhaps at Aunt Emma (Em) Frost's house in Arvada, Colorado. The family had arrived from Gate, Oklahoma, the previous spring and summer. Left to right: Jeanne, Charley, Buelah, Forrest, Martha, Arl Frost, Harold, and Emma Frost. *(Source: Maurie Craft Lang's family collection, permission by son Martin Lang)*

Fig. 8.2. The Craft family in Arvada, circa 1930. Left to right, front row: Martha, Jeanne, and Charley; middle row: Buelah and Maurie; and back row: Paul, Forrest, Cecil, and Harold. *(Source: Maurie Craft Lang's family collection, permission by son Martin Lang)*

Fig. 8.3. The Craft children in the yard of the rented Craft house in Arvada, Colorado, circa 1930. Left to right, front row: Buelah and Maurie; back row: Paul, Forrest, Cecil, and Harold. *(Source: Maurie Craft Lang's family collection, permission by son Martin Lang)*

Fig. 8.4. Charley and Martha Craft on their rented farm in Arvada, Colorado, 1930. Charley would have been only 58 and Martha 54 years old. *(Source: Maurie Craft Lang's family collection, permission by son Martin Lang)*

Fig. 8.5. Charley and Martha Craft with two of Charley's half sisters from North Carolina on the front steps of the rented Craft house in Arvada, Colorado, 14 August 1934. Left to right: Odella Lineback, Charley, Martha, and Virginia (Jenny) Robertson. Note that Charley's skin color had darkened, perhaps reflecting his declining health. *(Source: Maurie Craft Lang's family collection, permission by son Martin Lang)*

Fig. 8.6. Charley and Martha with relatives on the porch at the Craft house in Arvada, Colorado, 14 August, 1934. Left to right, front rows: Buelah, Martha, and Jeanne; back row: Forrest, Odella Lineback, Charley, Virginia (Jenny), Harold, Flossie (Paul's wife). Charley is very sick at this time, as shown by his skin color. *(Source: Maurie Craft Lang's family collection, permission by son Martin Lang)*

192

Because Charley had so much confidence in old friend Dr. Archie Dougan, who had retired to Kansas, he asked him to visit and to diagnose his illness **(Fig. 8.8)**. Dr. Dougan traveled to Arvada, Colorado, in the summer of 1934, stayed with Charley and Martha, and convinced Charley that he needed the operation.

The outcome of the operation is unknown. Whether the surgeon found heart blockage or some other debilitating disease is unspecified, but increasingly, Charley's health deteriorated. In his final days, he convalesced at home **(Fig. 8.9)**. He died of heart failure at 62 years of age in the fall of 1934, in the family's home with his dog Fritz at his side. It is not known, for certain, whether Charley Craft's hardships shortened his life. Nearly all of his Craft and Leinbach/Lineback relatives, however, outlived him. Most lived into their 70s or 80s.

Charley's final debt from his Oklahoma homestead was settled from his estate. On 26 June 1935, his estate paid off a $1,600 mortgage made in 1914 to the Federal Land Bank.

After Charley's death, Martha gave up the house in Arvada because she could no longer afford it and rented a small apartment. She did some baby-sitting and some sewing in order to support herself. She volunteered temporarily to work with the *Pillar of Fire*, a nondenominational, fundamentalist religious organization based in Denver, although she did not continue very long. It was seemingly to fulfill a deep desire by Martha to be "needed," according to Jeanne Baker (2002), which may help explain her close relationship with the Quaker church in Gate. Perhaps this observation also explains

193

much about Martha's life, her drive, and her willingness to bear extreme hardships.

At least twice, Martha came to North Carolina, probably about 1936 and 1946, to visit the Crafts and Leinbach/Lineback families. She would have been 60 and 70 years old, respectively, at the time, still active and still of bright mind. All of her own children visited her frequently in Denver and helped her travel some in her twilight years. Her granddaughter Jeanne Baker (2002) remembered going with Martha to visit museums and similar sites in and around Denver, taking the trolley that provided inexpensive intracity travel.

Martha's life had been filled with hardships, but she had not complained, a characteristic much cherished by the Craft family. She had been a strong-willed woman with high energy and a willingness to "make do." She was a perfect partner for Charley Craft. Martha died at age 76 on 6 May 1953 of an unknown illness. She outlived Charley by 19 years.

Fig. 8.7. Charley Craft in front of his and Martha's rented house in Arvada in the last year of his life, 1934. He would have been 62 years old and in declining health. *(Source: Maurie Craft Lang's family collection, permission by son Martin Lang.)*

Fig. 8.8. Dr. Archie Dougan and Charley Craft in Arvada, Colorado, 1933 or 1934. Charley had requested that his friend Dr. Dougan visit from Kansas to confirm his Colorado doctor's diagnosis at the hospital. *(Source: Maurie Craft Lang's family collection, permission by son Martin Lang)*

Fig. 8.9. This photograph was taken of Charley and his dog, Fritz, in Arvada, Colorado, immediately following Charley's hospital visit in late summer of 1934 and within weeks of his death. *(Source: Maurie Craft Lang's family collection, permission by son Martin Lang)*

The Rest of Buelah Craft and Leslie Carpenter's Story

Buelah had several suitors after the Craft family moved to the Denver area. Soon after her divorce from Leslie Carpenter became final, she married Bill Son, a railroad worker, in 1927. Her daughter, Jeanne, began using the name Son, believing that Bill Son was her biological father. Jeanne continued to assume that her last name was Son for the next 30 years. Bill Son, however, was neither her natural father nor her adoptive father. When Jeanne married Sid Baker in 1944, she learned that her mother Buelah had recently gone to district court and had her name legally changed to Vera Jeanne Son.[131]

Throughout most of Jeanne's life, she knew nothing about the circumstances of her birth in Gate. Bill Son's family had difficulty accepting Jeanne into the family. In fact, Jeanne remembered being treated differentially by the Son family and not understanding the reasons **(Fig. 8.10).** It is possible that Bill Son's family knew little of the truth about the circumstances of the Craft family in Gate.

Fig. 8.10. Seven-year-old Jeanne Carpenter Son stands in front of her stepfather, Bill Son, and her mother, Buelah, 1930. *(Source: Maurie Craft Lang's family collection, permission by son Martin Lang)*

In 1947 while visiting her Uncle Paul and Aunt Flossie Craft in Oklahoma City, Flossie's father, "Dad Newman," told Jeanne that her biological father was Leslie Carpenter, not Bill Son. He also told her that he believed Leslie Carpenter was still alive. He made no mention, however, of the circumstances leading up to

Jeanne's birth in Gate. Because neither Jeanne's mother Buelah nor any other family member would speak of the events surrounding her birth for so long, Jeanne felt that the subject was best left alone.[132]

In the 1950s, however, Jeanne's aunt and uncle Maurie and Martin Lang moved to Denver, and Jeanne visited with them often. Maurie began to encourage Jeanne to learn more about her father, and Maurie told her parts of the story that Jeanne had never heard. Maurie still had a contact with someone in Gate through a friend living in Denver. Maurie knew that Leslie was alive and well and where he and his family were living. Maurie also told Jeanne that her mother Buelah had once said, "You only love one man enough to have their child."[133]

Clearly, Leslie Carpenter had not died of syphilis— and in fact had not even had it! Tragically, Dr. Nylund in Gate had misdiagnosed the disease.

This information stunned Jeanne, who had no idea that her biological father, Leslie Carpenter, was even alive. In fact, Maurie told Jeanne that Leslie had been to Buelah's flower shop in Golden, Colorado, at least twice to ask to see Jeanne, but Buelah had refused each time. From the standpoint of Jeanne's childhood, this opportunity could have made a big difference for her, for while her stepfather's family was rejecting her, her biological father desperately wanted to see her.

Why Buelah chose not to allow Leslie to see his daughter is a question that can never be answered. Perhaps Buelah thought a meeting between Leslie and Jeanne might lead to embarrassment for her or the family. Maybe she thought a reunion would deeply hurt

Charley or otherwise change his close relationship with
his granddaughter Jeanne. Maybe Buelah just could not
forgive Leslie for being unfaithful to her. On the other
hand, perhaps she just could not accept the fact that so
many mistakes had been made in the aftermath of the
misdiagnosis.

Over the next 22 years, Jeanne tried to reason out
the situation. Meanwhile, she was working at a bank and
raising her own two daughters. Who was the father she
had never known? She had learned through Maurie that
her father Leslie and his family lived in Boise, Idaho.[134]

Finally, on a trip to see her own first granddaughter
in Canada in 1970, Jeanne decided to visit her father. She
had great apprehension about meeting him and his family,
wondering whether she would be accepted or rejected.
Gathering her courage, she stopped unannounced at her
father's house in Boise. He was on the carport when
Jeanne greeted him and told him who she was. Tears
welled up in his eyes as he hugged her and said, "Jeanne,
we have missed 40 years." Leslie introduced Jeanne to
his wife Lucy and family, and later during that first visit,
Lucy told Jeanne, "Leslie never got over your mother."[135]
(Fig. 8.11)

When Jeanne returned from Canada, she told her
mother that she had gone to see Leslie. Buelah's only
answer was, "Someday I will tell you the other side of the
story." But she never did.[136]

Leslie flew to Grand Junction, Colorado, in 1973
and stayed with Jeanne and her family a few days in
Glenwood Springs. Jeanne brought her daughters to meet
their grandfather, and he seemed very excited to know his

granddaughters. There was some concern among Leslie's family that Jeanne wanted something from him, perhaps an inheritance, but, gradually, trust grew between them. Jeanne found Leslie and his family to be kind and gracious. Leslie died in Boise 30 October 1992 at 90 years of age.

Fig. 8.11. Leslie Carpenter, as he looked when his daughter Jeanne first saw him in Boise, Idaho. "He was a sweet man. I only [knew] him for 15 years" (Jeanne Baker, 19 April 2003). *(Permission by Jeanne Baker)*

The Modern Craft Family

At the time of Charley's death in 1934, all of the Craft children were married, except Harold and Forrest.

All of the children remained close to Charley and Martha, although there were some repressed tensions between some of the siblings arising from the forced separation of Buelah and Leslie Carpenter. Throughout her life, Maurie blamed Paul for initiating the separation. Maurie had learned rather early on that Leslie had not had syphilis and had lived. Exactly when Maurie learned that Leslie survived is not clear, but through her connections with someone in Gate, she may have kept up with Leslie and his family throughout the years after the Crafts left Gate.

It is uncertain how Buelah felt toward Paul, as she never talked about the events that transpired around her relationship with Leslie. By at least 1930, Buelah learned that Leslie had lived, as he contacted her at least twice at her flower shop in Golden in efforts to see their daughter, Jeanne. A family photo of the six grown Craft children taken about 1933 showed Buelah standing beside Paul with his arm around her. Her body language seems to indicate some distaste toward Paul's show of affection **(Fig. 8.2)**, but the family did not remember that Buelah held any grudge against him. With this single possible exception, all of the Craft children got along extremely well and remained dedicated to one another throughout their lives. Buelah's nieces and nephews affectionately called her "Aunt Booty." When Paul was drawing up his will in the last years of his life, Maurie told him that he should leave something to "Booty" because he "owed her," according to Velma, Harold's widow (2002).

Paul Vachel Craft married Flossie Newman in 1922, and they lived most of their lives in Oklahoma City almost within sight of the State Capitol. They had no children. The Newman's were a well-to-do family, and it is likely that Mr. Newman was generous to Paul and Flossie, as he lived with them in his later years. Paul had a detached retina and lived on government disability and business investments, several of which were only marginally profitable. One of those was a soft drink enterprise that Harold Craft ran in Stillwater, Oklahoma. Flossie died 18 November 1973 in Oklahoma City, and Paul died 13 July 1977 in Denver, having outlived her by four years.

Soon after the family's arrival in Colorado, Charley approached the local judge who rented him his land in Arvada to request assistance in obtaining a divorce for Buelah from Leslie Carpenter. The uncontested divorce was granted in Jefferson County, Colorado, on 1 December 1926. Reverting to her maiden name, Buelah Florin Craft then married Bill Son, a railroad worker, in 1927 and moved to Golden. After Bill lost his job in the 1929 Depression, he went into a dairy operation with his father, selling milk to Coors for malted milk. Buelah and Bill had no children; Jeanne was Buelah's only child. Buelah opened a flower shop called *Son Flowers* in Golden, where she struggled to keep her flower shop going and renovate a piece of commercial property and a home in Denver, as well as maintaining acreage outside of Golden. She was much like her mother, determined, uncomplaining, and willing to take on difficult jobs. Buelah died in March 1993. Her daughter Jeanne married Sidney Baker, an engineer, and they had two daughters. Jeanne currently resides in Glenwood Springs, Colorado.

Harriet Maurie Craft became one of the earliest women aviators, flying bi-wing airplanes for fun and in air shows and even crashing one plane after hooking a barbed wire fence with the wheels during a take-off. Maurie married Martin (Marty) Lang, a professional baseball pitcher, in 1932. Although Marty struck out Babe Ruth, he quit baseball to become an industrial engineer. Maurie and Marty had two children, Martin (Marty Jr.) Charles Lang (b. 1934) and Martha Carolyn (Carol) Lang (Payne) (b. 1944). The Langs lived most of their married lives in Wichita, Kansas, and Denver. Maurie died on 24 August 1999 in Tucson, Arizona, at the age of 92.

Cecil Irving Craft graduated from Arvada High School and attended the Colorado School of Mines for two years, graduating later with a petroleum engineering degree from The University of Oklahoma. He married Ellen Magnelia Erickson in 1933 in North Platt, Nebraska. By 1940, he owned and operated a drink (pop) bottling plant there. Midway through WWII, he served as a lieutenant colonel in India. Cecil was elected Nebraska state senator in 1956, and he died 1 March 1966 while still in office. Ellen was appointed to fill out Cecil's senatorial term. She then ran and won the seat on her own, becoming an influential Nebraska state senator in her own right. The Craft State Office building was named after both of them. They had four children, John (Jack) Charles Craft (b. 1938), Cecil Irving Craft (b.1935), Thomas Erick Craft (b. 1946), and Susan Ann Craft (b. 1948).

After two years in the military, Harold Newby Craft married Velma Mae Kimball in 1942. Harold was a businessman all of his life, first co-owning with Paul Craft and operating a soft drink factory in Stillwater, then owning a snack machine operation, and finally buying, renovating, and renting apartments around Denver. Harold and Velma had five children, twins Paul Gale Craft and Harold Dale Craft (b. 1943), Charles Robert

Craft (b. 1945), Marilyn Maurie Craft (b. 1960), and David Martin (Topper) Craft (b. 1955). Harold died on 30 January 1999.

Forrest Emmanuel Craft married Bernice Campbell in 1937, three years after Charley's death. Forrest owned and operated a construction company. Forrest and Bernice had four children, Dean Herbert Craft (b. 1938), Ronald L. Craft (b. 1941), Linda Levonn Craft (b. 1948), and Forrest Wayne Craft (b. 1951). Forrest died on 21 March 1969.

APPENDICES

I. Interviewees
Charley Craft: The Life and Times of a
North Carolinian Turned Oklahoma Homesteader,
1872-1934

Harold Newby Craft

Charley and Martha Craft's fifth child and married to Velma Kimball, Harold was the principal source of information for this book. Interviewed several times between 1988 and 1999 at the family home in Wheatridge, Colorado, the author taped many hours of conversations with him. His memory was brilliant, and his recall of details from his earliest childhood was extraordinary. A robust individual with a friendly way, Harold was gracious and helpful despite the author's persistent and penetrating questions about the family's interactions. Harold died in January 1999.

Velma Kimball Craft

Harold's wife and mother to their five children, Velma provided details and new perspectives about the Craft family, even after Harold's death. She spent many hours with the author in 2002 going over photographs of the family and postcards from the early 1900s.

Harriet Maurie Craft Lang

Maurie was the third child and second daughter in the Craft family. She married Martin Lang, and she also had an excellent memory. During visits to the Lang family home beginning in the 1950s, Maurie provided stories to the author about the Craft family's homesteading in Oklahoma. Not until 1988, when she was 81, did the author begin seriously recording her comments and conversations at the Harold Craft family home, and her memory of facts was exceptional. Maurie died in August 1999.

Buelah Craft Carpenter Son

Buelah was the Craft family's second child and oldest daughter. Although the author first met Buelah in 1959 in Golden, he had only one opportunity to record her conversations in 1988 about her early childhood on the Craft homestead in Oklahoma. By this date, at age 85, she was showing signs of memory loss, but she was able to remember many details about the homestead and the family. Significantly, Buelah never talked to the author or her daughter, Jeanne, about the family's final days in Oklahoma. She died in March 1993.

Jeanne Carpenter Baker

Jeanne was the daughter of Buelah Craft and Leslie Carpenter. She believed that Buelah's second husband, Bill Son, was her biological father until she married Sidney Baker. She resides in Glenwood Springs, Colorado. She was Charley and Martha's first and their closest granddaughter because the family had been involved so much in her life. The author had many opportunities to talk with Jeanne beginning in 1959, but it was not until 1988 that he began to record her, along with her mother, Buelah, Harold, Maurie, and Velma, at the Harold Craft family home. Her story was integral to the complete family history in Oklahoma, and she was very forthcoming and gracious about explaining her and her family's deepest feelings during and after some of the family's most tumultuous times.

Wayne Lewis

Wayne was an 86-year-old long-time resident of Gate, Oklahoma, when the author first met him at the Gate Friends Church in January 2002. An avid local historian and genealogist, he accompanied the author to the abandoned Craft homestead site and provided invaluable details about landownership, prairie living, and the history of the Gate community.

Paul Wilburn Jones

Paul Jones was the author's 78-year-old first cousin in 2002 and a great-grandson of Junius Craft. Paul's grandmother Odella (Della) and Charley Craft were half-sister and -brother. Paul was responsible for renewing this author's interest in Charley's story in the 1980s by relating much of the family's oral history about Charley and his family. Although the author remembered many of the stories heard from his own father, Paul was able to fill in details, link things together, and help provide new perspectives derived through stories he had heard from his own mother and our grandmother.

Martha Leinbach

Martha was a double-second cousin to the author; her mother and his grandmother being sisters and her father and his grandfather being brothers. Martha prided herself in being the Craft/Leinbach/Lineback family historian. As the author researched Charley Craft's story, he visited

Martha in Winston-Salem in 1994 to obtain information about Charley's life in North Carolina. Although she was in her 80s at the time, she was able to provide a single newspaper clipping which led the author on a protracted and circuitous research effort to find Charley Craft's North Carolina child. Martha died in 1999.

Carl Sapp

Carl Sapp was a 98-year-old long-time resident of the Mt. Tabor Community and friend of the Craft and Leinbach/Lineback families. The author interviewed him in the spring of 2002. Carl did not specifically remember Charley Craft, but he remembered Charley's father, Junius, and stepmother, Martha Styers Craft, providing details about the last years of their lives. Carl died in April 2002, two months after being interviewed.

Charles Robert Craft

As Harold Craft's son and Charley Craft's grandson and namesake, Charles assisted the author in understanding Charley Craft's complicated financial dealings arising out of his homesteading efforts in Oklahoma.

Gary Stephen Lineback

This author's brother and surveyor/civil engineer, Steve Lineback, provided expertise in obtaining and interpreting the Craft family's property deeds and land transactions in North Carolina dating back to the 1890s.

Harvey Bailey

Harvey Bailey is a distant relative of Pleas "Plez" Bailey, a local black man who had a large influence on Charley Craft as a young man. Harvey provided information about his relative, using stories passed down in the family as oral history. He lives on some of the original Bailey property on Robinhood Road, just west of the Lewisville-Vienna Road.

Jerry Loafman

Jerry Loafman is the family historian for the Hicks family from the Pfafftown-Vienna-Lewisville area of North Carolina. He was instrumental in providing circumstantial evidence identifying Junius George as Charley Craft's son. Jerry also provided several photographs from the Hicks' family collection for this book.

Randall Carpenter

Randall Carpenter was Leslie Carpenter's 96-year old brother at the time the author interviewed him by phone in Idaho. Randall provided insight into how the Carpenter family dealt with the separation of Buelah and Leslie, when the Craft family left Oklahoma for Denver.

Theresa Hutchins

Theresa is a distant relative of Anne Ellen George Moose, Charley Craft's alleged North Carolina granddaughter, through Anne's mother, Lelia Barr. Theresa was instrumental in helping the author discover details about Anne Ellen's death in Seattle, Washington, in 1983 and obtain copies of her death certificate and Social Security application. Theresa is a police officer living near Mt. Airy, North Carolina.

II. EVENTS TIMELINE

Charles V. Craft's Events and Family Relations, 1814-1960

Year	Day/Mo.	Events (Relations)
1814	19 May	**(Stepfather) Rev. Daniel Doub** born (d. 1874)
1830	23 Mar.	**(Aunt) Theresa (Tessie) M. Craft** born (d. 3 Oct. 1890)
1842	21 Mar.	**(Father) Junius Irving Craft** born (d. 28 July 1918)
1850	23 Jan.	**(Aunt) Senia Ellen Craft (Whitman)** born (d. 14 Mar. 1922)
1866	24 May	**(Aunt) Theresa (Tessie) M. Craft** and **Rev. Daniel Doub** married
1869		**(Stepbrother) Boyd Vachel Doub** born (d. 1932)
1869		**(Uncle) John Tillet Craft** born (d. 27 Nov. 1942)
1871	25 May	**(Aunt) Senia Ellen Craft** and **Norman Eugene Whitman** married.
1871	21 Sept.	**(Father) Junius Irving Craft** and **(Mother) Jane Hariett Kimel** married
1872	*20 Oct.*	*Charles Vachel Craft born*
1872	? Dec.	**(Mother) Jane Hariett Kimel Craft** died
1874	23 Sept.	**(Father) Junius Irving Craft** and **(Stepmother) Martha Antionette Styers** married

1874		**(Stepfather) Rev. Daniel Doub** died
1875	7 July	**(Half-Sister) Madora Odella Craft (Lineback)** born
1875		**(Stepbrother) Boyd Doub** married **Mary Elizabeth (Lizzie) Lineback**
1876		**(Half-Sister) Buelah Craft** born/died to **Junius & Martha Craft**
1876	*4 Aug,*	*(Wife) Martha Ann Newby born (d. 1953)*
1877	5 Mar.	**(Half-Sister) Etta Amelia Craft (Lineback)** born
1879	28 April	**(Halfbrother) Calvin Russell Craft** born, died in infancy
1880	24 Nov.	**(Half-Sister) Virginia (Ginny) Craft (Robertson)** born
1881	19 Mar.	**(Half-Sister) Daisy Estelle Craft (Ensley)** born
1889	25 Jan.	(Halfbrother) **Samuel Irving Craft** born
1889	Spr/Sum	**Bill Lineback** and **Charley** went to Noblesville, IN, for the first time and worked in wheat
1890	Jan	**Charley** bought the Doub 12 from **Boyd Doub** for $42.
1890	3 Oct	**(Aunt and Stepmother) Theresa Craft Doub** died
1891	15 July	**(Half-Sister) Martha Blanche Craft (Livingood)** born
1895	13 Nov	**Charley** and **Martha Newby** married.
1896	9 July	**(Son) Paul Vachel Craft** born (d. 13 July 1991)

1902	27 Oct.	**Charley** and **Martha** in Indiana deed the Doub 12 in North Carolina as a Mortgage Deed to Junuis I. Craft for $120 and released on either 8 March or 8 Sept. 1911.
1903	18 Dec.	**(Daughter) Buelah Florina Craft (Carpenter, Son)** born (d. ? 1993)
1904	Fall	**Crafts** move to Oklahoma
1906	Spring	**Crafts** file for their relinquishment (Henry Fellow Memoirs, p. 25)
1907		Laurence (Laurence Tom Kersey) Friends Academy built (*Henry Fellow Memoirs*, p. 24).
1907	7 Feb.	Postcard from Maude Heneke asking how they like living there in Gate. (Heneke family soon moved in Northeast of the Craft place. He was apparently the neighbor who Harold describes.) Tape 4, p. 3.
1907	7 July	**(Daughter) Harriet Maurie Craft (Lang)** born (d. 1999)
1908	31 Jan.	**Eula Lineback** wrote **Buelah** to ask how **Martha**'s baby is doing, referring to **Maurie** (Tape 4, p.2)
1908	29 June	**Sam Craft** in North Carolina writes Paul Craft in Gate a postcard (Tape 4, p. 2)
1909	3 Feb.	**Martha** takes **Buelah** to Indiana on a train to settle father's estate. (Postcard to **Paul** from Chicago, note from "**Momma**" to **Paul**) (Tape 4, p. 1)
1909	12 May	**(Son) Cecil Irving Craft** born (d.1 Mar. 1966)

215

1910	8 Aug.	**Charley** receives a Final Receipt Record (a Certificate) on 120 acres in Beaver County, OK: N ½ of SW1/4 and NW1/4 of SE1/4 of Sec. 15, T5N,R28E
1910	22 Aug.	**Charley** mortgages the farm to Samuel H.Groves (First Trust and Savings Bank, Chicago) for $600 (Released 16 Oct. 1914)
1911	6 Mar.	**Charley** receives a Patent Record on his Homestead.
1911-12		Blizzards from December until April
1912	13 Feb	**Freida Lineback** writes postcard to **Paul** asking about **Cecil's** appendicitis (prior time) (Tape 4, p 2)
1912	12 April	Postcard from **Arl Frost** saying that "A 24-inch snow has not been gone a week."
1912	12 June	**(Son) Harold Newby Craft** born (d. 30 Jan. 1999)
1912	7 Oct.	**Charley** sells farm to W.E. and Cassia Pratt and A.B. Card
1912	28 Nov.	Gate Valley Star notes the "Craft Farewell." **Crafts** moved to Palacios, TX
1912	7 Dec.	**Charley** takes note on his land from Pratt, Pratt and AB Card for three payments of $933.33 each (total of $2,800).
1914		Gate School is built in Gate and competed with Laurence Friends Academy (Wayne Lewis)
1913-14		**Crafts** living in Palacious, TX
1913	13 Jan.	Postcard from **Arl Frost** to **Paul** in Palacious. "Almost a foot of snow here." Clear from card that **Charley** went ahead to Texas (Tape 4, p. 2)

1913	26 Aug.	**Frostie** and **Emma** "moving to Colorado right away. May be in our house by Xmas" (Postcard to **Paul**). (Tape 4, p. 3)
1914	Spring	**Bill Lineback** dies in Carmel, IN, only one week after arrival. Ellis Lineback family suspects rabies. Attended by Dr. Hershey. Died at Sherman Shields's home.
1914	15 June	**Charley** apparently released P&P&C from the sale of the Craft farm.
1914	Summer	The **Craft family** moves back to Gate from Palacios, TX
1914	15 June	**Charley** borrows $1,000 from Pittsburg Mortgage Investment Co. (Released 20 Nov. 1928)
1914	15 June	**Charley** borrows $140 from Pittsburg Mortgage (Released 15 June 1918)
1914	21 Oct.	**Charley** paid $600 to First Trust & Savings Bank (Chicago)
1914	13 Nov.	**(Son) Forrest Emmanuel Craft** born in Gate (d. 21 Mar. 1969)
1914	7 Dec.	**Charley** was supposed to have received second payment on $2,800 debt owed him, but had apparently moved back to Gate and had released P&P&C of the debt.
1915	9 Nov.	Wayne Lewis born.
1916	5 Dec.	Postcard from **Frostie** asking **Paul** how the well drilling is going. There is apparently an old Ford Rambler on the Craft farm (Tape 4, p.3)
1917	14 Feb.	**Charley** receives his Warranty Deed back from WE Pratt (handled in Matagorda County, TX)

1917	3 Oct.	**Charley** borrows $1,600 from Federal Land Bank (Released 28 June 1935)
1917	12 Dec.	**Charley** signs an oil and gas lease on 80 acres
1918	15 May	**Charley** pays off the loan of $140 from Pittsburg Mortgage Co.
1918	28 July	**(Father) Junius Erving Craft** died
1918		Postcard from **Paul Craft** in San Francisco to family inquiring about whether "you all are over the influenza now?" (Tape 4, p.2)
1920	12 April	**Charley** signs another oil and gas lease on the remaining 40 acres
1922	Feb.	**Charley** and Dr. Dougan visit North Carolina
1922		**(Son) Paul Vachel Craft** and **Flossie Alice Newman** married
1922	20 June	**Charley** mortgages the farm to State Bank of Commerce, Gate, for $1,000 (Released on 5 Sept. 1928)
1923	July	**(Daughter) Buelah Craft** discovers she is pregnant
1923	20 Oct.	**(Daughter) Buelah Craft** and **Leslie Carpenter** married (KS)
1923	26 April	**(Stepmother) Martha Antionette Styers Craft** dies in North Carolina.
1924	19 Feb.	**(Granddaughter) Vera Jeanne Carpenter (Baker)** born to **Buelah** and **Leslie Carpenter**
1924	March	**Charley, Harold, Buelah,** and **Jeanne** begin trip to Denver in open Ford touring car.

1924	*Spring*	**Martha** stays to sell farm equipment. (Wayne Lewis attends sale.)
1924	16 June	**Charley** and **Martha** give a Warranty Deed to State Bank of Commerce, Gate, for the Craft Farm for $3,000. Signed in Colorado.
1926	29 May	**(Daughter) Buelah Carpenter**, Plaintiff, files for divorce from **Leslie A. Carpenter**, Defendant, in Jefferson County, Colorado
1926	1 Dec.	Divorce decree granted to **Buelah Carpenter** from **Leslie Carpenter**
1927	19 Jan.	**(Daughter) Buelah Carpenter** married **Bill Son**
1928	5 Sept.	**Charley** paid $1,000 to State Bank of Commerce, Gate, $1,000 to release mortgage from 20 June 1922
1928	20 Nov.	**Charley** paid $1,000 to Andrew Jarnett, Executor, for Robert Andrews (Pittsburg Mortgage) to release mortgage from 15 June 1914
1932	3 June	**(Daughter) Harriet Maurie Craft** and **Martin Lang** married
1933		**(Son) Cecil Irving Craft** and **Ellen Magnelia Erickson** married
1934	27 Sept.	**(Grandson) Martin Charles Lang** born to **Maurie** and **Martin Lang**
1934	**Fall**	**Charles Vachel Craft died.**
1935	28 Jan	**(Grandson) Cecil Irving Craft, Jr.** born to **Cecil** and **Ellen**
1935	28 May	**Charley's** estate paid $1,600 to Federal Land Bank on mortgage made on 3 Oct. 1917

1937	19 June	**(Son) Forrest Emmanuel Craft** and **Bernice Campbell** married
1938	28 Nov	**(Grandson) John (Jack) Charles Craft** born to **Cecil** and **Ellen**
1938	7 May	**(Grandson) Dean Herbert Craft** born to **Forrest** and **Bernice**
1941	25 Jan	**(Grandson) Ronald L. Craft** born to **Forrest** and **Bernice**
1942	27 Nov.	**(Uncle) John Tillet Craft** died.
1943	26 June	**(Grandson) Paul Gale Craft** and **(Grandson) Harold Dale Craft** (twins) born to **Harold** and **Velma**
1944	23 Jan	**(Granddaughter) Martha Carolyn (Carol) Lang (Payne)** born to **Maurie** and **Martin Lang**
1945	10 Jan.	**(Grandson) Charles (Charley) Robert Craft** born to **Harold** and **Velma**
1946	13 Nov	**(Grandson) Thomas Erick Craft** born to **Cecil** and **Ellen**
1948	28 May	**(Granddaughter) Susan Ann Craft** born to **Cecil** and **Ellen**
1948	21 June	**(Granddaughter) Linda Levonn Craft** born to **Forrest** and **Bernice**
1951	30 June	**(Grandson) Forrest Wayne Craft** born to **Forrest** and **Bernice**
1953	6 May	*(Wife) Martha Anne Newby Craft died*
1956		**Harold** and **Velma** moved family from Stillwater, Oklahoma to Denver, Colorado.

1956   23 May **David Martin (Topper) Craft** born to **Harold**
        and **Velma**

1960   22 March **(Granddaughter) Marilyn Maurie Craft** born
        to **Harold** and **Velma**

REFERENCES

A History of Beaver County Pioneer Families. Vol. I, 1970, Beaver Co. Historical Soc., Inc.

A History of Beaver County, Vol. II, 1971, Beaver Co. Historical Soc., Inc.

A Short History of the Gate Friends Church, 1905-1985. 1985, Gate Monthly Meeting of The Friends Church.

Fellow, Henry C. *Account of Henry C. Fellow's "Little Historical Thesis," Written in 1942-43 in His 86th Year.* Recovered in 1980 and transcribed by Elaine A Maack (unpublished).

Kinney, Nellie Ethel Wilson. *Crafts of North Carolina.* July, 1985, Nellie Ethel Wilson Kinney (unpublished).

Maphet, Ernestine. *The Vigilantes.* 1978, Ernestine Maphet (self-published).

Maphet, Ernestine. *Gate to No Man's Land.* Date unknown, Ernestine Maphet (self-published).

Sage and Sod, Harper County, Oklahoma, 1885-1974. Vol 2. 1975, Harper County Historical Society.

ENDNOTES

[1] Nellie Kinney, *Crafts of North Carolina*, July 1985. Self-published.

[2] As told to Paul Wilburn Jones by his mother, Eula Lineback Jones, circa 1950s.

[3] Reflecting on discussions with his mother, Eula Lineback Jones, Charley Craft's half-niece, half a century later, Paul Wilburn Jones said (20 December 2001): *It was always my understanding that Uncle Charley's adoptive mother had a baby boy [about] his age, thereby supplying milk for Charley.*

[4] Conversations between the author and his father, Hiatt Lineback, circa 1970-80.

[5] Contemplating the role that Pleas might have had in her father's life, daughter Maurie Craft Lang, (1996) said: *And that was "Plez"—he was the black man that took care of Papa [Charley]. He just took care of him like—better than a lot of women would have. I don't know where he lived or if he lived (in the same neighborhood). I know that he was a black man and I know that Papa gave him credit for teaching him to shoot.*

[6] Harvey Bailey, interview, 2002.

[7] Charley's son, Harold (1988) described Charley's relationship with Pleas Bailey: *Dad often told us stories of going "coon hunting" with "Plez," who had some dogs. They would be out all night and Dad had some good stories to tell.*

[8] Conversations with the author's father, Hiatt Lineback, circa 1970s.

[9] Daughter Maurie Craft Lang (1996) struggled to explain why Charley seems to be estranged from his father and stepmother: *I wondered a lot since we talked [with the author] a year ago about why Charley's other [siblings]*

didn't insist on Charley coming back to the [Craft] house with them. You think his father's second wife [Martha Styers] was not agreeable to that, or what? I never could understand what the "bound business" had to do with anything you did only by verbal [agreement].

Paraphrasing from a conversation with Maurie Craft Lang (1995), this author transcribed from his notes: *That's something that Martha Leinbach [a family historian] and I talked about a little bit, too. She said that her mother [Charley Craft's half-sister] thought or told her that the bound boy or bound child was a legal adoption. That there probably was paper in the old courthouse which would have been in Salisbury [or somewhere], since Forsyth County separated from Stokes County. And so she said she always wondered if there wasn't legal paperwork.*

[10] All of Charley Craft's halfsisters married local boys and stayed relatively close to home. Della was the oldest and the one with whom Charley had the closest relationship, which was because they were closest in age and she best knew the details of his bound boy situation.

[11] Conversation with Ellis Hiatt Lineback, circa 1980.

[12] According to Bill Leinbach's daughter Martha, quoting from a telegram still in the family.

[13] As told by Ellis Hiatt Lineback to the author, 1955.

[14] Warranty Deed, *Deed Book 41*, page 70, Forsyth County Deeds and Records.

[15] Since Charley did not receive any of the Doub land as part of an inheritance, however, this indicates that he was not considered part of the Doub family. Just the fact that the Doubs insisted on Charley keeping his Craft surname indicates that they felt that they were simply raising him, as was the tradition of bound children of the time, and not fully adopting him. What was particularly unsettling to the other Craft children about the relationship was that

Theresa had suckled Charley as a baby and that Charley had worked diligently on the farm throughout his late childhood, adolescence, and early manhood. One would think there would have been an unbreakable bond between him and the remaining two Doubs. If such a bond ever existed, it apparently had loosened by this time.

[16] Buelah (1988) remembered Maurie going to research Charley's history in North Carolina: *Maurie [Craft Lang] has been down in North Carolina and followed through on things she was told. And [she] went out to the cemetery and to see that it was true. But I never have. Every time I get into that chest [Charley's layette], I [come to a dead end]. If somebody would pick it up [research it], we could find out a lot more. But that blanket chest [that now belongs to me] was Papa's layette. You know, I brought that back from North Carolina. I don't know. You work so far with it and then you don't get there [don't find out any more]. On the side of Papa's mother's family—her name was Harriett Jane—I was really looking for her parents or her grandparents. Harriet Jane Kimel was her name. I think her father's name was Demuth or something like that . . . the information on that I wasn't sure was dependable. You just ran into a [dead end] on it. In North Carolina at that time, there were quite a lot of people who worked for the North Carolinians and got very little compensation for it. The Civil War came long. [Papa] was born on the thirteenth of October and [his mother] died in December before Christmas.*

[17] To the best of this author's knowledge, there was only one breach in this unwritten family agreement. This breach occurred when Sam Craft's (Charley's halfbrother's) wife, Kathleen, spoke to Maurie (Charley's daughter) at a family picnic in Ellis and Della Lineback's yard about 1958. It was Maurie's last afternoon of a trip explicitly to

search the Forsyth County Clerk of Court files for answers about Charley's youth and his reasons for leaving North Carolina.

Kathleen asked Maurie whether she had had any luck finding anything at the courthouse. To this, Maurie replied that she had not. Kathleen then said, "You may never know the rest of your family." This statement stuck in Maurie's mind for the remainder of her life, as she realized that it had some sort of hidden meaning. Thirty years later, Maurie told this story to this author and asked whether he "knew what Aunt Kathleen meant." Although he knew, he could not break the pact. His reply was to turn the question around and ask her, "Do *you* know what Kathleen meant?" He then changed the subject.

Following Maurie Craft Lang's death in 1999, the last of Uncle Charley's children had passed away. On a trip to Morehead City, North Carolina, in April 2000, cousin Paul Wilburn Jones informed Charley's oldest granddaughter, Jeanne Baker, about some of the generalities of Charley's secret, more than 110 years after the fact. Although Paul did not know the details, he was able to convey the overall story to her. Jeanne was shocked.

Worried about how concerned Jeanne appeared to be about this information, this author gave the same information to Harold Craft's son and Charley's namesake and grandson, Charles Robert Craft, at the Craft reunion in Estes Park, Colorado, in June 2000. Again, neither Paul Jones nor the author knew many details of Charley's secret at that time.

[18] Original records, 1880 U.S. Census.

[19] Jerry Loafman, 2002.

[20] Buelah (1988): *Martha's mother [Rebecca] was from North Carolina, having walked along side a covered wagon to Indiana. Her brother was the first doctor in Indiana, called "Dr. Harold" by family members.*

[21] Daughter Maurie Craft Lang (1988) remembered a few things she had heard about her grandfather Gideon Newby back in Indiana: *[My mother's father, Gideon] was a handyman. He ran a sawmill and he was a kind of a jack-of-all-trades. He did clock work when they were having to cut the cogs out [of wood to make clocks]. He tended an orchard too.*

[22] This is the only surviving personal correspondence from Charley before 1900. Used by permission of Velma Craft.

[23] Velma Craft (2002) seemed to remember that there was talk of another child born to Martha and Charley: *I remember Harold talking about it, but I don't know what happened to it. But it didn't live very long.*

[24] Unpublished memoirs of Henry Fellow (1942-43) state: *Following a vacation trip back to Indiana [Carmel], we aided in the campaign to build a Friends Meeting House on the purchased lots [in Alva, Oklahoma].*

[25] Regarding his own successes at fundraising, Fellow's unpublished memoirs state: *Charles Brown went on two soliciting missions to England and brought back money for the Academy's building. I was sent to Phila[delphia] and the East on a like quest and brought back some $500 to $600. . . . I circumspectly and continuously addressed the conservative Philadelphia Friends with "thee" and "thou" and spoke of Friends meetinghouse or Friends School, and I never went away empty-handed. I received a gift of some twenty dollars for the Friends School at Tonganoxie and Will [William Whitaker, a Quaker friend, who had been less successful at raising funds from the same source] treated me to a glass of lemonade [apparently in acknowledgement of Fellow's superior fundraising ability].*

[26] Viewing a copy of the deed still in the family, grandson and namesake Charles Craft (2002) was surprised: *See, she [Martha] never went down there [to North Carolina to sign the deed]! Either someone signed it [the deed] for her or it was signed up in Indiana. It isn't notarized.*

[27] Researched in the Forsyth County Records office by Steve Lineback (1995), the deed reads: *[In] 1904, J. I. Craft deeded 12 Ac. to Wm. Parks. [Deed Book 74, pg. 65] Property was financed by J. I. Craft for $120 per Mortgage Deed recorded in Deed of Trust Book 43, pg. 583 on Aug. 30, 1904 and was paid off either March 8 or November 8, 1911.*

[28] Grace Smith in *A History of Beaver County* (Vol. II, 1971) describes the trip from Alva to Gate: *[The three families] chartered a railroad car and brought all our household furniture (from Indiana) to Alva. The men came on out and built a small house on the claim of Henry Fellow and filed on claims while the women remained behind [in Alva].*

[29] Dwight Leonard in *A History of Beaver County* (Vol. II, 1971) states: *In 1890, the Territory of Oklahoma was created and No Man's Land was included. Other sections of Oklahoma were opened about the same time, but new settlers did not start coming back into our area [Beaver County, the easternmost Panhandle county] until around the year 1903. By 1906, it was estimated that 40,000 people had come into the Panhandle. The last chapter in the turbulent history of No Man's Land was written in November, 1907 when Oklahoma became a state.*

[30] Fellow, again, states: *In the summer of [1904] Pres. T.W. Conway, Wallace Wilmot [?] and myself went to Woodward and through the courtesy of the real estate firm, James A. Moon, Realtors, were conveyed by team to Gate Valley and shown the prospective land. It was the year 1905* [contradicts a later quote of 1904] *that I filed on the N.W. ¼*

of Sec. 27-T28-R26. [This section of land is actually located in Woodward County, just on the edge of the Panhandle and just three miles east of the land that Charley Craft ultimately homesteaded.]

A section from "A Short History of the Gate Friends Church" found in *Semi-Centennial Historical Sketch of Kansas Yearly Meeting of Friends* (1985) states: *Having been somewhat inured to frontier conditions and feeling the call of the "West Land" for Christian service, your humble servant and wife [Henry and Melissa Fellow] filed on a claim in Gate Valley, Woodward County, Oklahoma, in the fall of 1904 and in the spring of 1905 Mack (sic) Smith, Charles Craft, John Card and families, recently from Indiana, likewise made their filings. Thus started the Friends settlement at Gate, twelve miles south of Englewood, Kansas.*

[31] A soddy was a house built in part by using pieces of thick prairie sod to build the walls and roof.

[32] Fellow's memoirs describe the people and the process: *... in the spring following [1905], the Smiths, Cards, and Crafts moved our household effects and theirs and filed on relinquishments for themselves. The Newbys, Whites, Allens, Browns, Kirkharts, Morgans and Newkirks came then; the Coppocks came in the next or three years and made a nucleus of a Friends settlement.*

[33] Grace Smith, in *A History of Beaver County* (1971) described her personal experience as her family moved from Alva to Gate: *We children attended school [in Alva] until February, when we came by train to Englewood [Kansas]. Ira Burch met us in a lumber wagon with straw and plenty of comforters to keep us warm. The Cimarron River was frozen over and he drove the wagon across on the ice.*

[34] Ernestine Maphet, *Gate to No Man's Land*, no date.

[35] Maurie (1995) stated: *They [the Crafts] homesteaded it [the farm]. But they could own it because the man that really homesteaded on it didn't prove up on it after he got it.*

[36] Ernestine Maphet in her book, *The Vigilantes* (1978), described the Panhandle in the late 1800s: *Out of Wichita, Kansas, came the announcement that the "Neutral Strip" [Cimarron Territory] was subject to be homesteaded. As in other places in the middle 1800s people began to migrate into the territory and by 1875 "Squatters" were making their homes here. These proud people lived in scattered shelters or dugouts with their families and their only protection of their squatter's rights was their own ability to eject the intruder.*

[37] Standing at the Craft house site on the homestead with the author in 2002 and looking south, Beaver County resident Wayne Lewis described the landscape: *This was the place where there was a stream . . . the lake spilling over and coming down this way. [Describing the intermittent stream through the Craft farm.] Now there was a [natural] lake here some 1,200 acres when it was full. Had catfish in it. The first lake was called Dishpan Lake and the big one was Gate Lake. When it would flow over, it would be 12 feet deep. [The owner has been] farming it now for three years. [It has dried up.] It didn't drain. Just hasn't rained. Called "playas" in this country.*

[38] Observation on the Craft farm by the author, 2002.

[39] Conversation between Wayne Lewis and his neighbor, Everett Maphet, March 17, 2002.

[40] Patent Record, signed 6 March, 1911, and filed in the Beaver County Records Office, 26 October 1914.

[41] Maurie (1996) expressed her childhood fears about the Cimarron River: *I know I can remember how I hated to [cross the Cimarron]. I wanted to go [to Englewood], but I*

hated to because they [the family] had to ford the Cimarron River and I wanted to be asleep when we got up there. You had to depend on the horses to swim you out.

Harold's recollection (1996) agreed: *You never knew whether the Cimarron River was high or whether it was low. There was no bridge to cross the river and you had to ford it. George Berends was on the east bank of the Cimarron River [2 May 1914], when they saw a flood coming from the other side of the river. There was a six-foot high wall of water, a mile wide. When they first saw the water coming, they ran for high ground, but were in water waist deep before they could get out. That's, like I told you, when you got to the Cimarron River, you never knew whether you were going to have high water or low water.*

[42] Harold (1995) described the fun he had trapping skunks: *I've trapped a lot of skunks, you know, with Bill Ness underneath the Ness house. It [was] a good place to trap skunks.*

[43] Velma Craft, 2002.

[44] *A History of Beaver County* (1971).

[45] Wayne Lewis (2002) also described the move: *Gate was a little country town out northwest of here [present site] and when the railroad came through, the railroad never went to a settled town. So it missed the town [Gate] and they [the town fathers] moved to the new town site about a mile from the old Gate site. So [new] Gate began in 1912 when the railroad came here. In most cases they just moved the buildings. And both churches [Quaker and Methodist] were built in the first year.*

Earl and Ada R. Kerns in *A History of Beaver County* (1971) also described the process of moving the town: *This [1912] was a very busy time as old buildings were moved to the new location and new ones constructed. Some of the buildings were too large and heavy to be pulled by horses and mules and it was necessary to use a winch.*

A.B. Card planned the new town site and sold lots. The new town grew rapidly and at one time was the largest town between Woodward and Beaver on the railroad.

[46] Granddaughter Jeanne Carpenter Baker (1995) remembered: *One of my earliest recollections, Grandma [Martha] Craft swears up and down that she never cooked using cow chips. No, no! Grandma used to say she washed [clothes by heating water outside in a large black iron pot] using cow chips [as fuel], but she'd never cooked with cow chips [as a fuel for her cook stove]. I can remember that.*

[47] Harold (1995) remembered the Craft house on the homestead: *It was a two-room [partial] dugout [or bank house]. As the family grew there was two rooms. The roof was raised on the dugout and two rooms [were] built on top of the two-room dugout. So it was a four-room house. Of course, being young, everything seemed larger than it does later on. And they weren't large rooms, but large rooms then [compared to the rooms in other houses in the area].*

[48] Pointing out some of the structures on early photographs of the Craft farm, Harold (1995) said: *See, here's the well [looking at a photograph taken after the house was gone]. And as it [the windmill] pumped water, it ran into a corner right in there and my dad had concreted a tank right in there. And then it would drain from there and then out there . . . where he kept his chickens alive. It was real cold water. The water would keep things cold. The water would be pumped from that well and come through a pipe into that [tank] and then the water from the bottom of it would be drained off. . . . My mom would keep butter, cream, etc. floating on a float [in the tank]. There would be a lid over the tank and that's what would keep things cold.*

[49] From recognizance of the Craft homestead site by the author and Wayne Lewis, 2002.

[50] Cory L. Morgan in *A History of Beaver County* (1971) says: . . . *a group of "Quakers" from Indiana and Iowa, emigrated to this prairie expanse. . . . There they filed their homestead claims, and, as such Quaker colonies have ever done when moving into a new area, they established a Sunday School and Meeting for Worship, assembling in their homes until a Meeting House could be provided.*

[51] Morgan again says: *[The Quakers] were able in that year [1905] to erect a building, on land given by Laurence Tom Kersey, an Iowa member, on his homestead two miles north east of Gate. In honor of the donor [of the land], this was named Laurence Friends Academy, and the building was both a meeting house and an academy for twenty years. . . . This school, which officially opened in the fall of 1905, was approved and fully accredited by the Territorial Board of Education, from the eight grade through the twelfth grade and was the only certified high school west of Woodward in the Territory.*

[52] Jeanne Baker, 1995.

[53] From various discussions between Craft family members and the author, 1985-2002.

[54] Pointing out the original site of the Academy to the author, Wayne Lewis (2002) said: *The Academy was here. A mile diagonally from the Crafts. Walked or rode? We walked to go to school, a mile and a quarter. Teachers lived with someone around in the area. No sign of the Academy anymore—not even a rock.*

[55] A handwritten note placed by Harold Craft on page 164 of his personal copy of *A History of Beaver County* (Vol. II, 1971) says: *Of interest: Buelah Craft Son, mother of Jeanne Baker, taught school one year at the "Berends" school. The only two students she had for ½ of the year was me [Harold] and Forrest Craft. I think 1921-22.*

[56] Howard Johnson, 2002.

[57] *Dots and Dashes*,.Vol. XXII, No. 4, Oct; Nov, Dec 1994

[58] The track was completed near Old Gate to Fogan, just north of Beaver. Laverne is located about 16 miles to the southeast of Gate along that railroad track.

[59] The storm probably occurred in April because the corn hadn't come up yet, so the hail didn't hurt it.

[60] Harold (1995) remembered: [*this lean-to on the barn is where]* . . . *the cattle got underneath to get out of the hailstorms.*

[61] Maurie (1988) remembered her experience with a great-uncle's tuberculosis: *[Grandma Newby] had one brother, Lewis. He was the one who lived in a tent in our yard [1909]. [He had] tuberculosis. He went back to Indiana and died. He did not live too long. Mom paddled [me] for . . . walking into his tent. And I was later diagnosed as a tubercular carrier and later Michelle, my granddaughter, was also diagnosed. Maybe I picked it up from Lewis's tent when I was only two years old.*

[62] Harold (1995) remembered some of the last cattle drives, probably by cattle buyers who were driving the cattle toward the railroad in Englewood, Kansas: *There were several cattle drives that drove right through past the house. I remember several of them [before 1920].*

[63] Maurie (1998) remembered her horse, Target, with both fondness and mild irritation: *I rode Target over there [to the swimming hole], you know, but I never went in [swimming]. I remember going under the tree. He was ornery, but he was smart too. But he was trying to brush me off.*

[64] Serial No. 09946.

[65] Beaver County Records Office, 2002.

[66] Wayne Lewis (2002) discussed the value of homestead land between 1905 and 1910: *[The land was probably worth] $30 per acre in 1905. My folks paid $35 per acre for*

some of theirs and that was a little later. A relinquishment. There was no land that had not been homesteaded by 1910. Very little by 1906.

[67] Wayne Lewis, 2002.

[68] Signed by Charley V. and Martha Craft on 7 December 1914 and recorded in the Beaver County Records Office Deeds Book 42, page 235.

[69] Signed in Matagorda County, Texas on 14 December 1912 and recorded on 9 January 1913 in the Mortgage of Real Estate Book 11, page 612, Beaver County Records Office.

[70] Recorded as a Mortgage of Real Estate, Book 11, page 612, Beaver County Records Office.

[71] Harold Craft, 1985.

[72] Colleen Claybourn, Matagorda County Historical Society, 2002.

[73] Original records, 1910 U.S. Census.

[74] Harold Craft, 1985.

[75] Original records, 1910 U.S. Census.

[76] Charley Parker, First United Methodist Church, Palacios, Texas, 2002.

[77] Recorded in the Beaver County Records Office on 6 August 1917 in Deeds Book 42, pg. 231.

[78] Beaver County Records Office, Mortgage Book 1, pg. 131 and Book 26, pg. 98.

[79] *Page 246, Misc. Book, Beaver County Records Office.*

[80] Recorded in Mortgage Book 38, page 511, in the Beaver County Records Office on 7 August 1917.

[81] Harold Craft, 1985.

[82] Interview with Harold Craft, 1988.

[83] As described by Maurie (1995): *You know, when we went back to Oklahoma from Texas they had to rebuild the barn. The tornado [destroyed it].*

[84] Harold Craft, 1988.

[85] Interview with Harold Craft, 1995.

[86] Paraphrased from a discussion between Harold and Velma Craft and Maurie Craft Lang, 1995.

[87] Interview with Wayne Lewis, 2002.

[88] Harold Craft, 1988, 1995.

[89] *A History of Beaver County Pioneer Families*, 1970, Vol.1.

[90] Paraphrased by Harold Craft from what he had read about Dr. Dougan in *A History of Beaver County. Interview with Harold Craft, 1995.*

[91] Paraphrased by Harold Craft from *A History of Beaver County Pioneer Families* (Vol. 1, 1978). Interview with Harold Craft, 1995.:

[92] Interview with Jeanne Carpenter Baker, 1995.

[93] Harold (1996) remembered baseball games between communities: *Baseball. Well, the high school played Rosston and different ones. Probably not [on] Sunday. Some Saturday afternoons.*

[94] Postcard from Martha Craft dated 3 February 1909.

[95] Another postcard from Martha on the same trip, dated 1909, but day and month obliterated.

[96] As told by Harold, 1995.

[97] Carl Sapp, 2002.

[98] Carl Sapp, 2002.

[99] Harold Craft and Maurie Craft Lang, 1985.

[100] Record of Deeds No. 160, Forsyth County.

[101] Carl Sapp (2002): *My oldest brother, Harv [Sapp], stayed with Old Man June Craft when he couldn't look after himself. He stayed with Old Man June for a good long while.*

[102] Harold (1995) remembered some of the details of the trip: *Well, we were still living in Oklahoma [when] he [Charley] went back there [to North Carolina]. He went back with an old doctor, Dougan. The old family doctor in Gate was from North Carolina too.*

[103] Wayne Lewis (2002) remembered Dr. Dougan's car: *He [Dr. Dougan] was one of the first folks in the country to have a car. I think he used a buggy before that, but he had a car by the time I was born in 1915.*

[104] Maurie (1996): . . . *Aunt Blanche [Blanche Craft Livingood, Junius's daughter] said to me one time, "What ever happened to the 10 or 20 acres that Sister Senia [Junius's sister] had. Who got that? Did Charley?*

[105] Forsyth County Record of Deeds, Book 230, Page 76.

[106] Mildred Hicks Dilworth, Keith Dilworth, and Jerry Loafman, 2002.

[107] Original document, 1920 U.S. Census.

[108] Jerry Loafman, 2002.

[109] This author obtained copies of her death certificate and her North Carolina Social Security application, proving she was one and the same.

[110] Certificate of Death, No. 34-00/204, Forsyth County Clerk of Court.

[111] Original document, 1920 U.S. Census.

[112] Leslie's 92-year-old brother, Randall Carpenter, remembered Leslie in a phone conversation with the author (2002): *Oh, Leslie was a good-looking boy who could put on a white shirt and a pair of clean pants and go to Gate. The girls all liked him and the boys didn't. One time at church over there, the boys turned his horse loose and poked it. The horse ran away with the buggy and tore it up. The boys were jealous of him.*

[113] Randall Carpenter, 2002.

[114] Jeanne Carpenter Baker, 2002.

[115] Jeanne Carpenter Baker, 2002.

[116] Jeanne Carpenter Baker, 2002.

[117] Jeanne Carpenter Baker, 2002.

[118] Wayne Lewis, 2002.

[119] Original document.

[120] Verified by Wayne Lewis, 2002.

[121] Harold (1995) described the family's source of information about Denver: *It just so happened in 1924, by my mother having a sister in Denver close by in a suburb of Arvada, that we had a place to land in Denver. They had visited us several times in Oklahoma. So we had a place to land.*

[122] Wayne Lewis (2002) described Dr. Dougan's wife: *She [Leona Long Dougan] was a saint. She was an excellent nurse without training, but compassionate.*

[123] As told to the author by Maurie Craft Lang's children, Marty Lang and Carol Lang Payne, 1995.

[124] Jeanne Baker, 2002.

[125] Wayne Lewis remembered attending the sale and described the conditions leading up to it (2002): *I can barely remember going to the sale [Craft farm]. But I don't remember anything else. This was not an unusual thing because there were a lot of folks selling and leaving [at that time]. Unfortunately, much of the land [around Gate] was mortgaged. And so when Oklahoma was set up as a state, a man named Bill Murray insisted that no corporation could own land in Oklahoma for more than five years—because a lot of people came out homesteading and mortgaged their land and walked off. They [the people who walked away] were selling their land to the mortgagor].*

[126] Deed Book 52, page 470, Beaver County Records Office:

[127] Paraphrased from the author's conversation with Maurie Craft Lang, 1995.

[128] Harold Craft 1988, Jeanne Baker and Velma Craft, 2002.

[129] Harold Craft, 1988.

[130] Velma Craft, 2002.

[131] Jeanne Baker, 2002.

[132] Jeanne Baker, 2002.

[133] Jeanne Baker, 2002.
[134] Jeanne Baker, 2002.
[135] Jeanne Baker, 2002.
[136] Jeanne Baker, 2002.

Index

Symbols

33rd Regiment, North Carolina 3

A

Alva, Oklahoma 27, 28, 31, 32, 33, 34, 35, 42, 228, 229, 230
Arvada, Colorado 175, 185
Arvada High School 204

B

Bailey, Harvey 211
Bailey, Please 7, 8, 224
Baker, Sidney 203, 208
Baker, Vera Jeanne Carpenter 63, 128, 153, 185, 193, 194, 238, 239, 240
learning about her biological father 199
marriage 203
move to Denver 173, 177
Baptist Church, Rosston, Oklahoma 160
Beaver City, Oklahoma 53
Beaver County, Oklahoma 28, 29, 32, 41, 43, 48, 50, 51, 53, 56, 60, 63, 65, 66, 71, 73, 107, 109, 114, 144, 148, 149, 163, 176, 180, 229, 230, 231, 232, 234
climate 82
wildfires 99
Beaver County Records Office 182, 236

Berends School, Gate, OK 68
Boise, Idaho 200
Bound boy 4, 5, 6, 8, 10, 11, 18, 225
Brookstown Road 136, 139, 143, 148, 150
Brown, A. (photographer) 135
buffalo chips 56

C

Card, A.B. 105, 106, 107, 108, 109, 111, 112, 113, 114, 179, 180
Card, John 31, 43, 65, 76, 77, 96, 97, 98, 109, 127, 128
Carmel, Indiana 15
Carpenter, Buelah Craft. *See* Craft, Buelah
Carpenter, Cornelius 160
Carpenter, Edith 162, 163
Carpenter, Leslie 160, 174, 202, 211, 238
death 201
diagnosis of syphillis 164
divorce from Buelah Craft 182
harvest work 161
meeting his daughter 198
misdiagnosis by Dr. Nylund 199
visit with his daughter 200
Carpenter, Lucy 200
Carpenter, Randall 163, 211, 238
Carpenter, Robert C. (Case) 160
Carpenter, Vera Jeanne 171
Cimarron River 41, 43, 44, 89, 230, 231, 232
Cimarron Territory 27, 28, 32, 33, 36, 88, 125, 231

241

G

Gambs, John 48
Gate, Oklahoma 33, 34, 35, 39,
    42, 51, 64, 209
  alcohol abuse 130
  commercial crops 99
  dust storms 81
  social problems 130
  spring weather 77
  stealing 132
  summers 79
  tornados 78
  winters 74
Gate Friends Church 209
Gate Lake 40
Gate Valley, Oklahoma 30
Gate Valley Star 52
George, Anne Ellen 17, 151,
    152, 153, 154, 155, 211
George, Cora. *See* Hicks, Cora
    George
George, Junius Levita 18, 151,
    152, 153, 211
George, Lelia Barr 151, 211
George, Salina 18, 151
Glenwood Springs, Colorado
    200, 208
Grand Junction, Colorado 200
Graves, Samuel H. 101, 106,
    115
Great Depression 182
Guilford College, Greensboro,
    North Carolina 125

H

hailstorm 81
Hand, Lawrence (Larry) 150
Hanzel. *See* Hanzl
Hanzl, Edward F. 168
Hanzl, Mary 168
Hanzl family 168

Harold, Dr. 21
Harold, Flavia V. 21, 50
Henekey, H.O. 130, 131, 133
Hershey, Dr. 14
Hicks, Cora George 18, 19, 151
Hicks, Thomas Henry 18
Hicks family 211
History of Beaver County, A 63
*History of Beaver County Pio-
    neer Families* 237
Home Comfort Range 56
Horse Creek 36, 40, 45, 95,
    129, 133
Hutchins, Theresa 152, 211

I

Indianapolis, Indiana 129

J

Jefferson County, Colorado
    150, 180, 203
Jones, Paul Wilburn 209

K

Kansas City Medical College
    125
Kerns, Ada R. 52
Kerns, Earl 52
Kersey family 30
Kimel, Harriet Jane. *See* Craft,
    Harriet Jane Kimel
Knowles family 30
krumholz 79

L

Lang, Martin (Marty) 199, 203
Lang, Martin (Marty Jr.)
    Charles 204, 239
Lang, Maurie. *See* Craft,
    Maurie

245

247

T

thresher, steam 96
tornadoes 78
Trade Street, Winston, N.C. 9
Trinity College, Greensboro,
	North Carolina 125
Tucson, Arizona 204

U

Union Center School, Gate,
	OK 68

V

Vienna Township 152

W

Walnut Cove, N.C. 8
Wheatridge, Colorado 207
wheat harvest 161
Whisenant, Mr. 75
Whitman, Norman Eugene 146
Whitman, Senia Craft. *See*
	Craft, Senia
Wichita, Kansas 204
Wichita Falls and Northwestern
	(WF&N) Railroad 53,
	75
Winston-Salem, North Carolina
	1, 4, 10, 65, 144
Woodward, Oklahoma 63, 163